MOUNTAIN ADVENTURES
IN THE MAURIENNE

About the Author

Andy Hodges was born in Wigan in 1967. He has been enjoying adventures in the outdoors since joining Cub Scouts in 1976. Learning to read a map and being allowed to tackle adventures were instrumental in nurturing a life long love for mountains. Student days allowed extended visits to the Provence region of France and he became a modern sports climber, while a summer holiday job saw him leading walking groups in the hills and mountains of the UK. He has been a volunteer member of Mountain Rescue for 16 years and is part of the Hasty Team, a fell running element of the rescue team.

Since discovering the Vanoise in 2004, he and his wife Sue have climbed, walked and cycled hundreds of miles of this beautiful region. There are hundreds more still left to be explored...

MOUNTAIN ADVENTURES
IN THE MAURIENNE

by
Andy Hodges

2 POLICE SQUARE, MILNTHORPE, CUMBRIA LA7 7PY
www.cicerone.co.uk

© Andy Hodges 2011
ISBN: 978 1 85284 621 3
Printed in China on behalf of Latitude Press Ltd

A catalogue record for this book is available from the British Library.
All photographs are by the author unless otherwise stated.

Advice to Readers

Readers are advised that, while every effort is made by our authors to ensure
the accuracy of guidebooks as they go to print, changes can occur during
the lifetime of an edition. Please check Updates on this book's page on the
Cicerone website (www.cicerone.co.uk) before planning your trip. We
would also advise that you check information about such things as transport,
accommodation and shops locally. Even rights of way can be altered over time.
We are always grateful for information about any discrepancies between a
guidebook and the facts on the ground, sent by email to info@cicerone.co.uk
or by post to Cicerone, 2 Police Square, Milnthorpe LA7 7PY, United Kingdom.

Warning

Mountaineering can be a dangerous activity carrying a risk of personal injury
or death. It should be undertaken only by those with a full understanding of the
risks and with the training and experience to evaluate them. While every care
and effort has been taken in the preparation of this guide, the user should be
aware that conditions can be highly variable and can change quickly, materially
affecting the seriousness of a mountain walk. Therefore, except for any liability
which cannot be excluded by law, neither Cicerone nor the author accept
liability for damage of any nature (including damage to property, personal
injury or death) arising directly or indirectly from the information in this book.

To call out the Mountain Rescue use the international emergency number
112 (118 in Italy): this will connect you via any available network. Once
connected to the emergency operator, ask for the police.

Front cover: West ridge of Pte. de Cugne (Route 18)

CONTENTS

Acknowledgements

I would like to thank my parents for making me stick at Cubs for a month; if I had left, I would never have learned how exciting and challenging the outdoors can be. Their trust in allowing me and two friends to go to the Lake District for a week when we were only 13 further instilled this adventurous spirit.

I would also like to thank my wife Sue for being my partner, not just in life but also on every route in this book. Some of the most spine-chilling episodes of our mountaineering careers have occurred in the Vanoise – these routes never made it into the guide!

To all my climbing and walking partners, from Scout days to present-day rescue 'missions', I offer my thanks and gratitude

I would also like to celebrate those volunteers who pass on their skills week in and week out, be they Scout or cadet leaders, teachers or youth workers. Their selfless commitment is rarely given the recognition it deserves.

Map Key

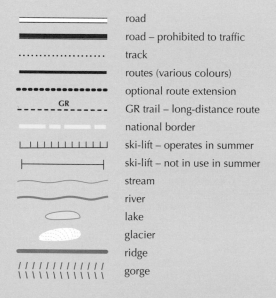

————————	road
————————	road – prohibited to traffic
··················	track
————————	routes (various colours)
●●●●●●●●●●●●●●	optional route extension
– – –GR – – –	GR trail – long-distance route
————————	national border
⊥⊥⊥⊥⊥⊥⊥⊥⊥⊥	ski-lift – operates in summer
⊢———————⊣	ski-lift – not in use in summer
∼∼∼∼∼∼	stream
————————	river
⬭	lake
⬭	glacier
————————	ridge
/////////// \\\\\\\\\\\	gorge

ⓢⒻ	start/finish	●	town/village
→	route direction	■	other building
🅿	parking	■	café
⬆	refuge/mountain hut	⸸	chapel/church
⋏	campsite	✳	place of interest
▲	peak	⊞	bike shop
⤬	col	�	fort
‖	bridge	·	spot height

Looking across to the Glaciers de la Vanoise from Plan du Lac (Route 49)

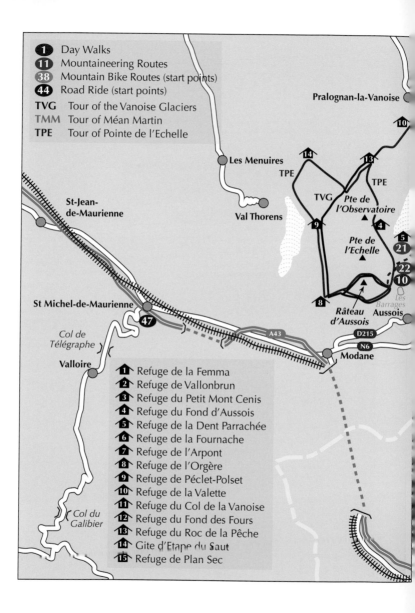

1   Day Walks
11   Mountaineering Routes
38   Mountain Bike Routes (start points)
44   Road Ride (start points)
TVG   Tour of the Vanoise Glaciers
TMM   Tour of Méan Martin
TPE   Tour of Pointe de l'Echelle

Pralognan-la-Vanoise

Les Menuires

St-Jean-de-Maurienne

TPE

TVG

Pte de l'Observatoire

Pte de l'Echelle

Val Thorens

St Michel-de-Maurienne

Col de Télégraphe

Valloire

Râteau d'Aussois

Les Barrages

Aussois

A43

D215

N6

Modane

Col du Galibier

1   Refuge de la Femma
2   Refuge de Vallonbrun
3   Refuge du Petit Mont Cenis
4   Refuge du Fond d'Aussois
5   Refuge de la Dent Parrachée
6   Refuge de la Fournache
7   Refuge de l'Arpont
8   Refuge de l'Orgère
9   Refuge de Péclet-Polset
10   Refuge de la Valette
11   Refuge du Col de la Vanoise
12   Refuge du Fond des Fours
13   Refuge du Roc de la Pêche
14   Gîte d'Etape du Saut
15   Refuge de Plan Sec

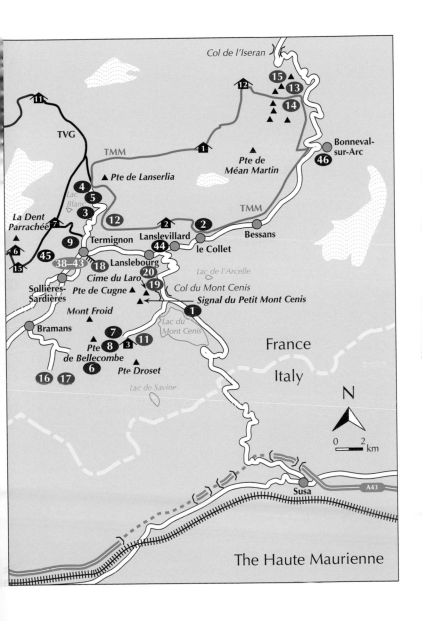

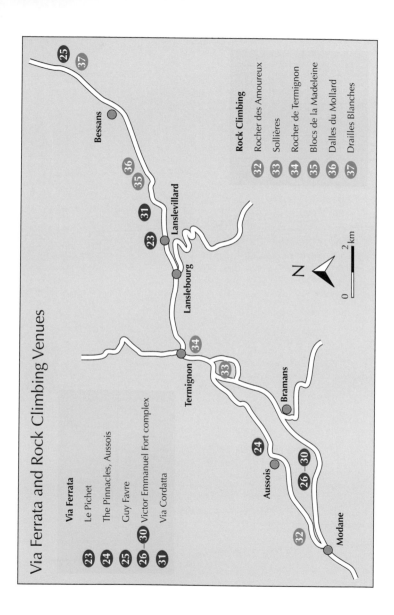

Via Ferrata and Rock Climbing Venues

Via Ferrata

23 Le Pichet
24 The Pinnacles, Aussois
25 Guy Favre
26–30 Victor Emmanuel Fort complex
31 Via Cordatta

Rock Climbing

32 Rocher des Amoureux
33 Sollières
34 Rocher de Termignon
35 Blocs de la Madeleine
36 Dalles du Mollard
37 Drailles Blanches

Bessans
Lanslevillard
Lanslebourg
Termignon
Bramans
Aussois
Modane

N

0   2 km

INTRODUCTION

Where do French mountain guides go for their holidays? I once asked a guide this question, while standing on the summits of the Domes du Miage in the Mont Blanc range, and he pointed to some rose-pink-tipped summits in the far distance. 'La Vanoise,' was the reply. And so began an adventure to discover a range of mountains steeped in history, modest in altitude and of breathtaking beauty. The Vanoise massif is a beautiful range of mountains bounded by the valleys of the Maurienne and the Tarentaise. The Maurienne valley is over 60km long, towered over by peaks of staggering symmetry straight from a child's

drawing of mountains. Many figures from history and mountaineering legend have trod through its forests and along its ancient tracks; yet the valley is somehow forgotten by the British mountaineering fraternity, despite having been at the heart of the early days of Alpine exploration. Now is the time to rediscover the Maurienne.

The Maurienne valley in the Savoy region was well known to European travellers; for millennia it was the main route from north-western Europe to the cultural centres of Italy. The English Romantic landscape artist JMW Turner was sufficiently inspired by his crossing of the Col

The Upper Maurienne Valley from the top of the Guy Favre via ferrata

du Mont Cenis to record the experience in a masterpiece, 'The Passage of Mont Cenis' (1820). The valley is also one of those believed to be central to the most famous of Alpine journeys, Hannibal's crossing of the Alps. His supposed route into Italy is now a pleasant half-day's walk to a far-reaching viewpoint. The valley also once formed the main route from Lyon to Milan and was part of the Spice Road between these two important cities – the village of Termignon had a chapel dedicated to *Notre Dame de Poivre* (Our Lady of the Pepper).

The French–Italian border in this area has shifted many times and there are nearly 30 fortresses in the valley, evidence of the many border conflicts. (Today, the Victor Emmanuel Fort Complex forms the focus of a series of breathtaking via ferratas described in this book.) In 1805 Napoleon Bonaparte ordered the construction of a road from the valley to aid his invasion of Italy. Throughout the mid-1800s the Dukes of Savoy fought long and hard here to maintain their sovereignty, as Savoy was a contested region between France and the Kingdom of Italy, under Victor Emmanuel.

The explorer Edward Whymper devoted a chapter of *Scrambles Amongst the Alps* to the ingenuity of the Fell railway and Frejus tunnel, both engineered to cross the Alps from here and in World War II fierce battles were fought to gain control of the road. The famous Maginot (or Alpine) Line, built to defend the French border, ran

through the valley and on many of the routes in this guidebook you will see the remains of fortifications and evidence of the front line.

So why have so few British mountaineers heard of this once well-known area? Perhaps it is because it lacks the highest peaks – nowhere is the 4000m contour reached – and has fewer glaciated summits than the higher and more famous Alpine regions. But this only makes it perfect for the connoisseurs of mid-grade mountain adventures, those wanting challenging routes and those wanting to mix and match their mountain activities.

The valley offers some of the finest modern **via ferratas** in France, routes specifically designed for sport, with reliable and well-maintained equipment taking direct lines up soaring cliffs and into the deepest of gorges. **Walks** and **scrambles** allow real summits to be reached from the valley in a day, with views reaching to the highest mountain giants in the distance, and **mountaineering** journeys allow the high summits to be reached without tackling glaciers. **Cyclists** will find themselves surrounded by Alpine giants familiar to any Tour de France follower, Col de l'Iseran, Col du Galibier and Col de la Croix de Fer amongst them. Nor will **mountain bikers** be disappointed, with waymarked trails threading through the forests and ski lifts to take the sting out of long climbs. Plenty of **rock climbing**

The view down into the Maurienne valley from near Lac de l'Arcelle (Route 1)

venues cater for everyone climbing from V Diff through to the higher E grades.

This guidebook is broken into sections according to interest and is written for someone visiting the region for a couple of weeks to explore and enjoy a number of mountain activities, maybe with different companions. The aim is also to ignite an interest in this beautiful region and encourage you to return for more mountain adventures in the future.

GEOGRAPHY

The Maurienne valley forms the southern side of the Vanoise massif and has two very different aspects. The southern side of the valley has developed as a ski area for winter sports and has a number of different ski stations, each opening its lifts on different days in the summer to make walking and mountain biking more accessible. Tranquillity is maintained on the other days. Access on this side of the valley is much more open and well-behaved dogs are welcome. To the north is the Vanoise National Park, offering peace and seclusion amid unspoilt surroundings.

Sitting on the French–Italian border, the Upper Maurienne (Haute Maurienne) has a southern boundary bordering the Italian region of Piedmont. Its northern border is less pronounced, as the massif of the Vanoise blurs the boundary with the Tarentaise valley. These two valleys, the Haute Maurienne and the Tarentaise, border the national park to north and south, while the Gran Paradiso National Park borders the area to the east. The Maurienne valley, carved by the Arc river, stretches for over 60km in length but the Upper Maurienne comprises the region between Modane and the highest summits overlooking Bonneval-sur-Arc and climbing to the Col de l'Iseran.

There are a number of recognised long-distance routes that pass through the valley or use it as part of a circuit. The most famous trek must be the GR5, which wends its way from Geneva to Nice and traverses the valley side for a few days of its journey. A less well-known and more recent route is the Via Alpina. This is a family of long-distance paths stretching across the Alps and crossing numerous national borders. The longest is the Red Trail, which at 161 stages is a mammoth walk; two of those stages, stages 123 and 124, pass through the valley, as the route heads south to Monaco.

THE VANOISE NATIONAL PARK

The northern part of the Maurienne valley gained national park status in 1963, the Parc National de la Vanoise (PNV), and was inaugurated in 1965 at the base of the Monolith at Sardières. It was the first national park in France and shares a boundary with the Italian Gran Paradiso National Park, the two parks becoming twinned in 1972.

Although the PNV is quite compact, covering 520km², in combination with Gran Paradiso it forms the largest nature reserve in western Europe at over 1250km². The peripheral zone around the reserve acts as a buffer to further expansion and adds a further 1450kms² of managed environment. The 600km of footpaths allow plenty of exploring within the park and the extensive network of paths in the peripheral zone more than doubles this, guaranteeing both a diversity of routes and solitude on all but the most popular routes. The national park designation has preserved the area from extensive development and protects the rural nature of Alpine agriculture. Compared to national parks in the UK there are more restrictions on activities, in particular:

- wild camping is not permitted. The only camping allowed within the park is lightweight tents next to refuges during July and August. There is a fee payable, which includes the use of the refuge facilities.
- all rubbish must be carried out; rubbish may not be left at the refuges.
- dogs are not permitted at all.
- flying (even using a paraglider) is prohibited.
- no mountain biking is permitted (with only one route exception).
- no fires are permitted.

The national park attracts over a third of a million visitors each year but many of these will be skiers enjoying the famous resorts of Val d'Isère and Tignes. In summer it is quieter on

Enjoying the view of the glaciers from Mont Froid (Route 7)

paths and roads, but has sufficient infrastructure to make backpacking and trekking enjoyable without the need to carry many days' supplies at a time.

GEOLOGY

The Maurienne valley was carved out long ago by an enormous glacial system. Its numerous tributaries formed the long side valleys leading into the main Arc valley. Many of these valleys still have glaciers in their upper reaches but these are retreating at an alarming rate and some will be lost in the coming decades. Climate change and glacial retreat are more apparent here than in most other parts of the Alps.

The rock here is mainly metamorphic and consists of reasonably well compacted schist and gneiss on the upper slopes. Conglomerate features in the valley, especially around Sollières where climbing on the localised pudding stone can be as much a lesson in geology as sport.

Near Sardières are two particularly unusual geological features, the Monolith and the Microlith. These impressive fingers of rock reach for up to 90m into the sky and host some challenging rock climbs within the capability of reasonably experienced climbers. The towers were formed by the dissolution of the surrounding beds of gypsum, leaving behind the limestone pillars.

WILDLIFE

The more remote valleys and high Alpine pastures of the Haute Maurienne are a haven for wildlife. The bouquetin (or ibex) population of the higher valleys is of national importance and their population is growing steadily. Animals from here are also being used to repopulate other mountain areas in France. Bouquetin are magnificent animals that move in herds and are easily identifiable from their dark brown coats, muscular build and iconic horns. Chamois are also in abundance and are likely to be encountered above the treeline on mountain slopes. Smaller than bouquetin, with longer legs and shorter horns, they will frequently be seen clambering among rocky outcrops and grazing on seemly barren slopes.

Bouquetin above l'Ecot

Marmots will be heard before they are seen. Their shrill alarm calls echo around the valley and these members of the rodent family can be

KEEPING SAFE AROUND THE PASTOU

Not strictly wildlife but an animal almost certain to be encountered is the *pastou*. These are large, white dogs that roam the mountainsides with flocks of sheep. Their role is to protect the flock from predators and threats, so they will be interested in your presence. The advice from the National Park is reprinted below.

A pastou coming to investigate

- Keep your distance, making a wide detour around the flock.
- Remember these dogs are guard dogs, don't try to pet them, feed them or do anything they might misinterpret as a threat.
- Behave calmly when passing them; avoid loud noises and sudden movements – this is probably particularly important if you have children with you.
- If one comes towards you stand still and allow it to work out what you're doing, avoid eye contact as dogs interpret eye-to-eye communication as a challenge. Walking away calmly and quietly is very effective.

seen standing atop rocky outcrops on sentry duty. An adult marmot will weigh around 5–7kg, and they live in communes of two or three generations. Once used for meat, fur and medicinal purposes, marmots are now a protected species. They hibernate during the winter and can be seen from late April onwards once the snow starts to melt. One particularly pleasant place to observe them is from the veranda of the Femma Refuge, although any open sunny mountainside will host any number of marmot family groups feasting on berries.

Less frequently seen are the large birds of prey. Golden eagles and bearded vultures live in the mountains and may well be seen soaring on the thermals. Ptarmigan and black grouse (tetras-lyre) also populate the mountains, along with nutcrackers, choughs and snow finches.

Lizards may well be spotted basking on rocks in the sun from Easter onwards, along with a whole host of butterflies and insects.

PLANTS AND FLOWERS

The Alpine meadows are a riot of colour in the summer months, and a lazy picnic amongst the multicoloured carpet of wild flowers can

Alpine gentian

Oeillet Negligée

Edelweiss

Mix of Alpine blooms in the high pastures

form the centrepiece to a relaxing 'day off'. Many of the flowers will be familiar to keen gardeners; others will be recognisable to even the least skilled flower spotter. Edelweiss can be spotted in sunny open places high above the treeline. Great splashes of white St Bruno's lily and a range of anemone, Alpine gentians and campanulas are frequently discovered on the high mountains, while in the valleys orchids are also found in damp spots. The meadows near Bonneval-sur-Arc and l'Ecot are carpeted with orchids, polygonum and dianthus in the summer months.

Trees are limited to the lower slopes and many walks are above the treeline, but the forests of Arolla Pine will provide welcome shade on valley walks and rides. These trees regularly live to over 600 years but are slow growing and as a result are vulnerable to deforestation. Careful management of the forests is very important, and the wood is popular with artisans because it has a good grain and is easy to work with. The larch is another commonly seen tree growing abundantly in the upper valley. It is unique in the conifer family as it loses its needles each winter.

HISTORY

Since the earliest of times the Maurienne valley has been occupied by human beings, and there is ample archaeological evidence stretching back to the Bronze Age and earlier. Much of this early history is explained in the museum at Sollières. The valley has served as a thoroughfare for travellers since Roman times, if not earlier. It is possible that it was the route Hannibal took to cross the Alps in 218BC on his famous journey, although no definitive archaeological evidence has ever been found of his crossing anywhere in the Alps. The route, via Col Clapier (Route 4), was still used as a main thoroughfare into the 16th century but once a more suitable route had been forged, over the Col du Mont Cenis, this old route fell into disrepair.

The region's economy has always been a mixture of agriculture and transport/tourism. The first road suitable for motor vehicles crossing the Alps was the Mont Cenis road. This was an improvement on the magnificent road constructed in the early 19th century on the orders of Napoleon to ease traffic over the pass to Italy. The modern-day road takes the same line, and the uniform gradient and sweeping curves make the 700m climb a joy, even on a bicycle. Technical innovations in transport were also tried and tested in the valley. The Fell railway, which was built from Saint-Michel-de-Maurienne to Susa, was described by the English illustrator, climber and explorer, Edward Whymper, as 'a marvel'.

Roman remains in Susa

This used a system to climb steep slopes, a precursor to the funicular railway; it followed the road for the main part, with an ingenious third rail placed in the centre of the track. The rail was 'gripped' by two wheels to allow a train to climb much steeper gradients than normal. Once over the pass, the descent to Susa was protected from avalanches by long covered sections. This was such a severe descent that the brake linings had to be replaced after each descent! Remains of these sections can still be seen next to the road today. The railway was an experimental undertaking and was dismantled when the railway tunnel at Frejus was constructed. This tunnel was started in 1857 and the two teams of tunnellers shook hands on 26 December 1870, with the first train travelling in September 1871.

Because of its strategic transport importance, the region has had a strong military presence. The House of Savoy has its origins in Sardinia and in the early 19th century its lands stretched from Lac Léman to the Mediterranean. The Victor Emmanuel Fort complex near Modane is the most striking feature of their reign in the region. The forts were built to repel invasion and each is named for a prominent member of the House of Savoy. The frontier has changed repeatedly (the most obvious example of this is to be found on the slopes of Cime du Laro, Route 19).

During WWII the strategic importance of the valley was not lost to either side. The subterranean fort

One of the many war memorials recording the great losses suffered in the valley right through the war

complex near Modane (part of an extended Maginot line built by the French during the military build-up in the 1930s) is a sober reminder of the conflict that came to this beautiful valley. The vicious weather conditions must have made the desperate battles for the high ground on Mont Froid, Pointe de Cugne and Petit Signal du Mont Cenis in April 1945 even more difficult. Footage in the museum at the Pyramide du Mont Cenis of the French soldiers receiving American rations in the snow shows just what the conditions must have been like.

ART AND CULTURE

The Maurienne was the road to and from Italy for those taking part in Grand Tours, and this has inevitably left its creative mark, with Baroque architecture and design particularly in evidence. Indeed, one church in Lanslebourg has been converted into a museum of Baroque architecture and artwork. Many other churches and chapels in the valley were designed in this style and are often open for visitors. A number of artisans throughout the valley also encourage visitors and sell direct to the public. The glass-blowing workshop at Avrieux and woodworkers at Sollières welcome visitors and sell unusual pieces made on site. Many dairies give guided tours (usually in French) of milk and cheese production, and also offer 'vente directe' for great prices and an opportunity to see

the source of such wonderful food. The local cheeses are of international renown and a key ingredient in many a picnic lunch.

Folklore abounds in the mountains and the Haute Maurienne is no exception. In or near Bessans many statues and paintings feature a four-horned devil. According to folklore a local man, Joseph, was contracted to build a bridge over the Arc. He fell behind in his work and was worried that he might end up imprisoned for failing to fulfil his commitment in the allotted time. The Devil appeared and made Joseph an offer that in return for his assistance the Devil would be allowed the soul of the first to cross the bridge. Joseph readily agreed and the bridge was duly completed on time. On the day of the opening, a troop of soldiers were approaching the bridge, led by a small local boy. Knowing what would happen to the boy if he was first to cross, Joseph's wife chased a goat onto the bridge. The goat saw the Devil and, mistaking him for another billy goat, charged him. His horns pierced the Devil's skull and the Devil escaped, never to be seen again.

Another tale gives an ancient account of the formation of the Chasseforêt glacier. 'Chasse forêt' translates as hunting forest, and this tale begins with a group of herdsmen tending their herds and flocks on the high mountain pastures and forest land. While they were engrossed in milking the cows and goats a beggar

A typical lunch high in the mountains, Dents des Ambin in the background

woman approached and asked for some milk. The men refused and sent her away with some strong words. She cursed the men and vowed they would regret their decision. That evening it began to snow. The snow continued to fall throughout the following days, steadily covering the pasture and forest. Eventually they were covered by such an accumulation of snow it began to turn to ice, putting the pasture out of reach of the herdsmen. The curse is said to have cut those pastures off for ever.

A more recent tale features Flambeau, a dog who throughout the 1930s delivered post to the fort high on the summit of Mont Froid. For ten years he made his way each day from Lanslebourg to the fort with the military mail and then returned home. In

pride of place in Lanslebourg high street is a memorial stone to this epic journey and faithful canine postman.

In this area, pride in traditional ways of life is very evident. Traditional dress is celebrated and hospitality centres on the fabulous local produce. There are many local shows and festivals celebrating all things agricultural and rural. Highlights include a wonderful community re-enactment of the Nativity in December at Bessans, the National Accordion Festival in Termignon in January, and a five-day husky dog sled race (le Grand Odyssée) throughout the valley in January. Any of these would add interest to a winter ski holiday. The summer festivals include a week-long astronomy festival, taking advantage of clear skies and the minimal light pollution to star gaze. The French national holiday on 15 August is cause to celebrate food and farming, with festivals and events throughout the valley. Sheep shearing and herding are demonstrated, along with dances and traditional dress parades. A growing mountain sports festival in August encourages novices and children to try a range of outdoor sports in collaboration with the local mountain guiding bureaus. The local tourist offices produce a free weekly newsletter outlining the upcoming events.

TRAVEL

The Maurienne valley is served by very good transport links, and travelling to the valley by public transport is perfectly feasible. Modane serves as the gateway to the upper valley and has a railway station with links from Paris and Turin, served by the TGV. The journey from Paris to Modane is around 4hrs, and by taking the Eurostar from St Pancras to Paris the journey can be both quick and environmentally responsible (without the complex baggage limits of airlines). Buses and taxis are readily available from the station into the upper reaches of the valley.

The A43 motorway enters the valley on its way to Turin and probably is the transport link many people will use. The favoured route is Calais-Reims-Dijon-Lyon-Chambéry-Modane. This avoids Paris and its associated traffic problems. In 2010 the motorway tolls were around €70 each way. A reasonable travel time from Calais is 10 to 11hrs. Taking an afternoon crossing and driving to the

Lanslebourg in bloom

Champagne region will break the journey. Troyes is a beautiful medieval town with a pedestrianised town centre and countless Tudor-style buildings. The next day's journey is then around 6hrs and makes for an afternoon arrival in the valley.

Budget hotel chains Formule1 and Etap offer good value, basic accommodation when you are travelling, and you can arrive any time as you can swipe your credit card at the door to gain access to your room. This means you can travel further later into the evening, but make sure you pre-book online.

Viamichelin is a useful route-planning website. It has information on the tolls for motorways and speed cameras; it also allows you to print out plans with the motorway signs included, which is of great help to the less confident co-driver.

On a Saturday in school summer holidays a good portion of Europe is travelling through France, and you would be well advised to avoid being part of the masses if at all possible – queues of an hour or more at booths for the Péage (toll roads) are not uncommon. The credit card lanes seem to move quicker.

Flying is also an option and there are a number of airports within 2 to 3hrs of the valley. Lyon, Turin, Chambéry and Geneva are all within striking distance, and the smaller airports offer quick check-in and arrival procedures, so you can be on the road in a hire car in no time.

Dent Parrachée from the Bellecombe road in winter. Perfect easy ski touring and snowshoeing abounds

Camping Mélezes: a peaceful and shaded site that makes a perfect base camp within easy walking distance of Termignon village centre

WHEN TO GO

The Maurienne valley is an outdoor adventure wonderland and offers winter sports for all, including renowned ski touring in late springtime. Snowshoeing is also popular right up until mid- to late May when the road passes begin to be opened up. What might be considered UK winter conditions will prevail in the higher mountains into June. The summer season really begins in July and extends through to late September. Early season snow will lie on the upper mountains in July and bare ice will be all that remains from late August. Almost all the routes in this guide will be snow and ice-free from mid-July onwards.

One event to bear in mind if planning a visit in July is the **Tour de France** cycle race. If the route follows the valley then there will be very heavy road congestion and all camping facilities will be fully booked.

ACCOMMODATION

Termignon is a reasonably central base for the Haute Maurienne. It is a quiet village situated about halfway along the valley, meaning you can easily access the climbing and via ferratas lower down the valley, the side valleys, the national park and the upper valley. The village has a tourist information centre (which posts a three-day weather forecast in English updated daily and has free internet access), an ATM, a new supermarket and petrol station, *cave de vin* selling many local wines, local produce

27

shop, equipment shop, a few bars and a couple of restaurants, along with a few fabulous cheese shops.

There is an abundance of self-catering accommodation available at Termignon's new apartment complex. These are clean, well-appointed apartments only finished in 2006. The view from the pool/gym area is a breathtaking vista of la Dent Parrachée.

There is a great campsite in the village offering two venues, one by the river in the shade and the other slightly higher in the sunshine. Site fees are very good value: in 2009 it cost slightly over €10 per night for a large pitch, a car and two people. It is clean and has plenty of hot water throughout the day. (You don't need to worry about grabbing a shower before the hot water runs out!) A little van selling bread and croissants signals its arrival with a cheerful beeping at 8.30 each morning.

Lanslebourg is the largest village after Modane and offers plenty of choice of accommodation. It also has a number of banks, equipment shops, restaurants and other shops (including a pharmacy).

Modane is a large town, and most people will pass through on their journey to the upper valley. There are two supermarkets, one at each end of town; both have petrol stations. There is an interesting range of shops including an organic supermarket, l'Esprit Vert, which also stocks a small range of vegetarian foods (an uncommon find in France

28

and a welcome one for any committed vegetarian in a group).

There are plenty of other campsites and rental accommodation throughout the valley – they are similarly priced to Termignon and offer quiet sites in picturesque surroundings.

MOUNTAIN REFUGES

The range of refuges in the mountains is very welcome whether as a base for a multi-day adventure, a single night as a launch pad to a summit or just for a welcome drink or spot of lunch. Many of them are owned by the French Alpine Club (CAF), while others are owned by the national park (PNV) and some are privately run. Costs are broadly similar but do vary from hut to hut, with *demi-pension* (three-course evening meal, dormitory bed and breakfast) costing around €40 in 2011.

There is a certain refuge etiquette which should be observed when staying in mountain huts. If you transgress these unwritten rules you can expect scowls and displeasure from the guardian!

First, and probably most important of all, is to pre-book. Turning up on spec means the hut may already be full, although the guardian is unlikely to turn you away it could mean you spend the night on the floor of the dining room with a blanket, in the woodshed (as happened to a friend in Austria) or in a corridor. None of these

The Vallonbrun Refuge nestled into its hidden valley with Dent Parrachée in the distance (Routes 2 and 49)

are particularly appealing options; a simple phone call can avoid such discomfort. It is possible to book huts further in advance via tourist information offices or via email from the CAF website and this is recommended in the height of summer, especially at weekends.

On arrival remove your boots in the porch/entrance hall. Put them in a pigeon hole (or whatever storage is present) and put on the clogs or slippers provided (or put on your own if you have decided to carry them). Then report to the guardian. Never enter in your boots – you will be scowled at (or worse) and it will instantly identify you as a novice and foreigner to mountain huts. The guardian and his/her assistants spend a lot of time keeping the refuge clean and will not welcome muddy footprints across their dining room floor.

If you have a British Mountaineering Club (BMC) or Austrian Alpine Club (AAC) reciprocal rights card present it to the guardian as you register for a reduction in fees – these are only usually accepted at Club Alpin Français (CAF) huts. Tell him/her your plans for tomorrow as you will be placed in a dormitory with people needing to get up at a similar time. (This is more of an issue when you are climbing and therefore need to get up at 4am or even earlier!) It is also worth being aware that there are no single-sex dormitories; they are all mixed.

At this point you will be asked whether you want evening meals and may be allocated first or second sitting if it is really busy. Vegetarians need a good sense of humour as evening meals often consist of eggs and something or pasta and sauce – tell the guardian of any special dietary requirements when you book in. It is also possible to self-cater and huts carry a range of implements but charge for the use of the stove and gas.

Lights out is usually relatively early (9 or 10pm); sort your kit out well before then. When you arrive take wet things to the drying room then organise your other kit: lay out your sheet sleeping bag, find your headtorch, wallet and other belongings. You will be the most unpopular dormitory resident if you start rummaging for things when others are trying to sleep.

Pay your bill before you go to bed. The guardian is usually very busy in the morning and you might waste

a lot of time waiting for him/her to be available, while everyone else is setting off. Ensure you have cash as very few huts take credit cards.

Don't forget to check the drying room before you leave; it could be a long trek back for anything you've left behind!

LANGUAGE

French is the language of the region, but Italian is also spoken as the region has had long-standing links with Italy; indeed 'ciao' is the standard greeting in the upper valley. English is spoken in tourist information centres but not necessarily by all staff. Younger members of staff often have a smattering of English but fluent English speakers are few and far between. The proprietor of Bar Marine in Termignon has a good

Typical signposting

Rescue is professional and efficient; make sure you have sufficient insurance cover

command of English and makes great efforts to welcome English visitors. As always, a game attempt in French is welcomed and the long tradition of catering for travellers throughout the ages means visitors are invariably welcomed and helped. A French phrase book will be a worthwhile investment! You are entering French France.

INSURANCE AND RESCUE

The European Health Insurance Card (replacement for the E111, forms are available online from Department of Health) allows access to the same standard of healthcare as a French national; this is not free at point of delivery like the NHS so good insurance

is also required. Insurance needs to include mountain rescue cover and helicopter evacuation. The two most popular options are Snowcard or BMC. To access BMC insurance you need to be a member of the BMC, if not then the membership fees will need to be taken into consideration which will add to the costs. Austrian Alpine Club (AAC) membership also includes annual rescue and repatriation insurance cover with no age limit. Snowcard insurance allows cover to be customised; if you have house contents cover then possessions are probably already covered so it is possible to purchase medical only or medical with cancellation cover, which is significantly cheaper with Snowcard. If you are a couple then you only pay

31

1.6 times the single person's premium too. Don't forget to photocopy everything and keep it in a waterproof bag.

Make sure the appropriate Mountain Rescue phone numbers are in your mobile before you need them. This will make dialling them in the case of an emergency much easier than trying to dial a long number under extreme stress with cold fingers in the rain or snow.

- European Emergency: 112 (118 in Italy)

Be aware, too, that in many parts of the mountains the phone network connects to the stronger Italian signal so a call to French Mountain Rescue may well be via the Italian emergency services.

Helicopter communications
Do not wave to a helicopter. To indicate that help is needed hold both arms up in a Y shape (see below). To indicate that no help is needed hold one arm diagonally up and the other diagonally down.

International Distress Signal
(only to be used in an emergency)

- **Six blasts on a whistle (and flashes with a torch after dark)** spaced evenly for one minute, followed by a minute's pause.
- **Repeat until an answer is received.** (The response is three signals per minute followed by a minute's pause.)

Helicopter Communications
These signals are used to communicate with a helicopter.

help needed

help not needed

 raise both arms above head to form a 'V'

raise one arm above head, extend other arm downward

Calling Mountain Rescue
In an emergency the mountain rescue (secours en montagne) can be called on **112** (**118** in Italy).

Note Mountain rescues must be paid for – be insured.

MAPS AND NAVIGATION

The French IGN 'Top 25' 1:25,000 maps are excellent. They identify the main paths in easy-to-see red, and more difficult sections are marked as red dots. They are sold at supermarkets and many other shops and cost around €9 each. Alternatively, they can be purchased online before you visit and there is now the option of a laminated version. (This isn't available in France, just in the Aqua3 online map shop.) Termignon is one of those places that is on the join of three maps, so three maps are needed to cover the whole area. An alternative is the 1:50,000 map (the Carte de Randonnées A3: Alps Vanoise) which clearly identifies waymarked walking routes, climbing sites, via ferrata venues and mountain bike areas.

1:25,000 maps

- 3534OT Les Trois Vallées Modane
- 3633FT Tignes, Val d'Isère, Haute Maurienne
- 3634OT Val Cenis Charbonnel
  The most recent editions of these maps show the extent of glacial retreat in a different colour.

If you are bringing a GPS, ensure it is programmed to datum WGS 84 and the grid system to UTM/UPS otherwise all grid references will be inaccurate. Don't forget to reprogramme it to UK settings on your return or the same problems will occur back in the UK.

Unlike the UK, paths are waymarked and signed to a high degree.

A friendly sign with an old walking boot being put to good use!

The signage usually gives information in times rather than distance, and these seem to be calculated with a similar formula to Naismith's Rule of 5km per hour. The red-and-white flashes on rocks, walls and buildings will become familiar friends, and the small cycling symbols will also be a welcome aid to route finding.

WEATHER

Weather forecasts are posted at tourist information offices, usually in French with a simpler version in English. These are updated daily and are for the coming night and next two or three days. They are generally accurate but be aware that they are based on Bourg Saint Maurice to the north and so need to be slightly adapted, particularly the timing of weather fronts approaching. You can get them by phone; the current phone number is listed on the weather reports. If you

The summit of Pointe de Leche and Dent Parrachée in the background (Route 21)

are staying in a refuge, the guardian can be a good source of information and advice on local conditions.

The sun can be a significant hazard; your sunscreen should be at least SPF15. Solar radiation at 1800m is more than twice that at sea level.

Good quality sunglasses are another must. If you wear spectacles, Optilab may be worth investigating for prescription sports sunglasses at prices not far off 'normal' frames and lenses. Photo-chromatic wrap-around glasses are great for all-day use in a variety of weather conditions. Remember, too, that the solar radiation is still there when its overcast.

CLOTHING

The weather in the Alps can change very dramatically. Snow can fall at any time of the year, even in August. Valley temperatures can drop to 5°C overnight in the summer. Equally, they can rise to over 30°C in the daytime. Therefore a fairly adaptable range of clothing and equipment is required. Given fairly accurate weather forecasts, it is possible to travel light by choosing appropriate equipment for the given weather. There is always a risk with this strategy, but by choosing some of the real lightweight kit available pack weight can be minimised, something which is really worthwhile when walking at higher altitudes.

For a day walk below the snow-line the following ought to be perfectly adequate:

- 30 litre rucksack
- Paclite Gore-Tex jacket
- softshell trousers (if the forecast is inclement)
- trekking trousers – with zip off legs (if forecast is good)
- Merino-blend socks
- boots – lightweight Gore-Tex lined or a tougher mountain boot depending on the terrain to be encountered
- wicking top – either long sleeve or T shirt
- mid-weight fleece
- lightweight fleece top
- wide-brimmed sun hat
- stiff-peaked water-resistant fleece-lined hat
- gloves
- good quality sunglasses – wrap-around style
- Buff (microfibrous, multi-functional headwear)
- sunscreen and lip salve
- small first aid kit
- trekking pole(s)
- 2 or 3 litre drinks bladder
- lunch
- emergency kit – small head torch; mobile phone; insurance documents; money; passport; gaffer tape; GPS
- map and compass
- guidebook
- camera

WET WEATHER ALTERNATIVES

With such a range of activities on offer, there is usually something to do. For a rest day, or when the weather has taken a turn for the worse, there are a number of alternatives.

The **Maison du Vanoise** at Termignon is an interpretation centre

Crossing a simple snow slope is still likely to need crampons (Route 22)

Mini-golf Parrachée

that allows you to understand the traditional lifestyle of the valleys and high mountains. One of the highlights is a model of a typical marmot colony enabling you to see exactly where the little critters go when the lookout whistles! The 3D virtual flight through the national park is a new technological attraction which combines a Google Earth type of projection with a large screen and a joystick control. Free internet access is also available, which may be useful for gaining longer term weather forecasts and keeping in touch. Downstairs is the tourist office and outside are the weather reports and an ATM.

The pyramidal visitor centre at the **Lac du Mont Cenis** is another interesting place to develop an understanding

of the area. It has displays of old farming methods and a section on the battle front of the valley during World War II. A short film (in French) gives an impression of the struggle the mountain troops faced. There are some written English explanations and a useful audio guide in English to help you understand the exhibition.

The **mini-golf** on the road out of Lanslebourg is popular; although the owner insists it is 'serious', it is a favourite with children. The **Biathlon d'Eté** (summer biathlon) centre at Bessans has a permanent summer course for roller skiing, which is like cross-country skiing without the snow. Equipment (including safety pads and helmet) can be hired locally and a day ticket purchased. Instruction is available and rollerblading is also welcome. Courses are colour-graded and surfaced in a smooth tarmac. Falls are inevitable, so jeans, or at least long trousers, are recommended.

The **high ropes adventure courses** (*parcours aventure*) at the Redoute Marie Thérèse near Modane and another on the road to Bellecombe from Termignon are sure to be a big hit with children (and those who enjoy thinking they're still ten years old).

There are numerous small artisans offering their wares: glassmaking, pottery and 'artisan du bois' abound and vary in style from beautiful to the more acquired taste. A visit to **Bois s'Amuse** in Sollières offers you a range of very reasonably priced wooden toys and ornaments.

Susa is a small Italian town 'over the pass' from Lanslebourg and was an important staging post for the journey from Lyon to Turin. It has a host of **Roman remains**, including an amphitheatre, triumphal arch and remains of the old wall and aqueduct. On the road over the pass, there are the remains of the covered Fell railway that forms a chapter of Whymper's *Scrambles in the Alps*.

Should you be in the area, then the refuge and restaurant at **Col de l'Iseran** has a small exhibition of WWII memorabilia and a gift shop. This is the highest point of the Tour de France when it passes through the area, and you are sure to see road cyclists climbing to the summit of the col.

A fabulous visit for fans of the Winter Olympics must be the **Olympic Museum** in Albertville, about 1¼hrs from Haute Maurienne. The town makes for a pleasant wander, particularly the old town. The parking in the town centre is very cheap, €2–3 for up to 4hrs. The museum has a host of outfits and artefacts on display and a very interesting short film (with English subtitles) explaining the build-up to the games. Another section has some slightly disturbing reflections on how politicians have hijacked the games for their own ends. A very reasonable entry fee and minimal souvenir shop make you feel that you are welcome to come and enjoy the values of the Olympics.

Crossing the Col du Galibier to explore the walled town of **Briançon**, the highest town in Europe, is another option. The old town and its maze of streets will be busy on a wet day but there are a number of forts that provide guided tours and a respite from wet weather. Further down the valley is **L'Argentière-la-Bessée**. This small town has successfully transformed from an industrial town into what may be described as an outdoor capital. It has a white water canoeing course and hosts numerous climbing competitions, as well as being home to the largest ice axe in the world, which stands outside the *mairie* (town hall). Many of the roads and streets are named after famous mountaineers, so a walk around the town may well turn into a who's who of classic Alpine mountaineering. Nor

37

should you miss the chance to visit the old capital of Savoy, **Chambéry**, with its elephant statue in the middle of town (a celebration of General de Boigne's exploits in India rather than an indication of Hannibal's passing through the region). The large market on Saturdays, the old town architecture and Dukes' Palace encourage an amble through the maze of backstreets and alleyways. The title of capital of Savoy is also claimed by Saint-Jean-de-Maurienne, which is home to the Opinel knife factory, a French classic. The factory houses a small shop offering a wide range of knives and household tools, all of the highest quality.

Further afield, a long day out to **Chamonix** can fulfil all your gear-shopping dreams. Towards the end of July the shops all have a huge clearout sale aimed at the French holiday market. The Quechua outdoor equipment supermarket at Saint Gervais has more incredible bargains. Chamonix has an interesting museum in the centre of town and a (very expensive) cable car trip up Aiguille de Midi is literally breathtaking, at around 3500m. It is always fun to plonk yourself at a pavement table and wonder just why people are wandering around in spotless outdoor kit in the middle of town.

The Pas de la Beccia with the frontier barbed wire still visible on the skyline (Route 19)

The road trip will be 2hrs or more each way.

Air sports are another option. **Tandem paragliding** is available in Termignon and pleasure flights can be booked from the Sollières airfield. For current information and advice, ask at the tourist office in Termignon.

USING THIS GUIDE

Timings

Timing is a very personal thing. It is easy to become demoralised by being unable to keep up with signpost times in France, only to find you are quicker than them once you are 'tuned in' to the hills (that is, fitter and acclimatised!). The route timings in this guide are based on the times it took the author to walk, climb or ride these routes. He doesn't stop very often (but doesn't race either), so add stoppage time as required. The times here are for the 'round trip': the shorter routes assume no acclimatisation but the more serious routes assume you have completed easier routes and are acclimatised.

Gradings

The origins of the gradings naturally differ from activity to activity. Here are some rules of thumb.

Walks

Walk grading is based on the author's perception of difficulty. Some of the routes assume that a level of acclimatisation has been achieved; this is

especially the case with longer routes. The walks are not technical inasmuch as there will be no scrambling involved and hands will not need to be used. There are a couple of routes (Routes 5 and 8) where there is a level of exposure, but this is limited to paths following ridges from a safe distance. Some routes are quite time-consuming and will require a whole day, while others are short rambles suitable for the whole family. In the UK, the author walks around 4km an hour and adds about a minute for 15m of ascent, and the timings given for the routes in this guidebook are based on this.

Mountaineering Routes

These routes are 'full on' mountain days. Many involve scrambles typical of those found in the UK, routes following exposed ridges with significant height gain. Virtually all the routes will require a reasonably high level of hill fitness, scrambling/mountaineering skills and acclimatisation. Grading is difficult to decide: the harder routes fall into traditional Alpine grades while the easiest routes are probably best described as rough walks. In this guide, Alpine grades and the author's impression of UK scramble grades have been used. It is worth bearing in mind that these routes are often much longer than scrambles in the UK, which will influence the grade as moving quickly is an important aspect. UK climbers are renowned for taking too much equipment and therefore moving too slowly.

The table below gives some general guidelines.

Scramble	UK climbing	Alpine	UIAA climbing	Verbal description
-1				Rough paths, paths may be exposed in places.
1	Easy	F	I	The occasional use of hands will be required. Paths are exposed.
1+				Hands will need to be used more frequently. Trekking poles are a hindrance. Some steep sections involve simple climbing moves.
2	Moderate	PD-	II	Some sections may need to be climbed as pitches. Considerable exposure will form part of the route. Steep terrain will be encountered for long periods. Rope may be required.
3	Difficult	PD	III	This type of route will involve exposure on steep ground, and most parties will move roped together for sections of these routes. Solo climbing will require considerable confidence and skill as a fall could easily be fatal. These routes will be long and need stamina and acclimatisation.

Via Ferratas

In France the Alpine grading system has been adopted. The grades bear little resemblance to those for mountaineering but follow the same sequence. The length of the route and the altitude are also important considerations.

- PD (Peu Difficile): these routes are straightforward and are often designed to encourage children to enjoy via ferratas.

- AD (Assez Difficile): more challenging and steeper routes requiring previous experience.

- D (Difficile): harder routes which demand fitness and a good head for heights. Vertical sections and significant exposure.

- TD (Très Difficile): much of the route will be vertical with overhanging sections and deliberately challenging features such as monkey bridges.

Climbing towards the ski station – the gradient is reasonable but it takes time! (Route 39)

Mountain Bike Routes

Many of the routes follow the published routes from the local tourist office. The routes are graded in a format similar to those used for ski runs:

🚵 Green: simple routes suitable for families and for those unfamiliar with cycling.

🚵 Blue: more challenging routes with greater height gain.

🚵 Red: quite challenging routes needing stamina and previous experience, as some sections are technically demanding. Significant height gains will need acclimatisation to the altitude.

🚵 Black: very difficult routes only suitable for technically accomplished riders with high levels of fitness.

Following the main ridge on la Turra de Termignon with Dent Parrachée looking down (Route 12)

1 DAY WALKS

These walks have height gains from 200m to over 1000m and vary from a couple of hours' ramble to full days in the high mountains. They will help acclimatisation in the early days of a visit before tackling the higher summits, although many are challenging days out in their own right. They give experience of walking in the higher mountains of the Alps and will reward the determined walker with breathtaking vistas. These routes require a modicum of navigation skills (although they generally follow good paths, usually waymarked and signed), proper walking clothing and equipment and an awareness of mountain weather. Snow can fall any time of year above 2500m; the weather forecast will be invaluable in helping you to plan accordingly.

The higher Alps are an area to extend existing experience and skills, while the lower walks enable even the least experienced walker to encounter spectacular views of the high mountains. Walkers without a reasonable level of experience and skill should seek guides from the Bureaux des Guides in the valley, or sign up with one of the guided walks offered by the tourist offices and outdoor shops.

Looking down the Maurienne valley towards Bramans from the Lac Blanc path (Route 3)

ROUTE 1
Lac de l'Arcelle

Time	3hrs
Distance	9km
Ascent	200m
Map	3634OT (Val Cenis)
Start	GR 0335 5014
Parking	Shortly after the Femma farm and fromagerie on the main road to Italy.

This is a short and fairly level walk, starting off at 2000m, which follows good farm tracks and footpaths, with only a couple of navigation points. As this walk is popular with less regular walkers, it is unlikely to be secluded on a sunny day. Beautiful reflected views of the high mountains make the lake a fantastic spot for lunch. Previous winter visitors will enjoy working out which ski runs they've skied down in the snow.

Drive up the road from Lanslebourg signed 'Italy' until the Femma farm is passed on the right (in summer it is a *fromagerie* that is open to the public and a perfect place to pick up some local cheese for lunch). Parking is on the left in a small lay-by near a farm track; the footpath sign here indicates no vehicle access along the track. Take this track, passing under a few ski draglifts, and begin to gently gain height.

After about 45mins the bubble lift top station and restaurant, **Le Vieux Moulin**, will be visible beneath the track. Keep on the most obvious track, shortly crossing the ravine of **l'Arcelle Neuve**, where the track makes a sharp V to follow the contours. As the path exits the ravine a small footpath on the right indicates that the lake is 35mins away. This path is fairly level and briefly gains a vehicle track to climb uphill. A wooden signpost (with the writing on the far side of the finger post) before

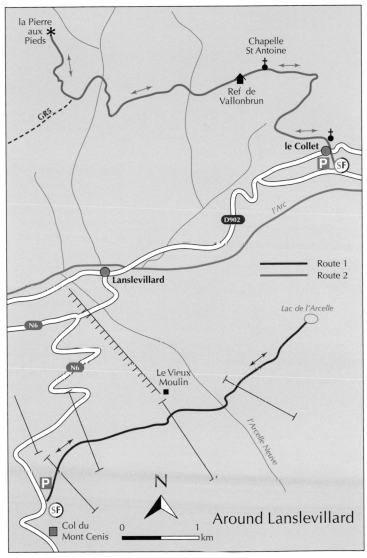

la Pierre aux Pieds

Chapelle St Antoine

Ref de Vallonbrun

GR5

le Collet

P SF

l'Arc

D902

Lanslevillard

N6

Route 1
Route 2

Lac de l'Arcelle

N6

Le Vieux Moulin

l'Arcelle Neuve

P

SF

Col du Mont Cenis

N

Around Lanslevillard

0   1
km

Lac de l'Arcelle and the Glaciers de la Vanoise make a beautiful lunch spot for an easy walk

a second uphill section indicates the lake is nearby. The footpath leads to the **lake**, which appears suddenly. This ramble will take about 1¾hrs in total.

The far-reaching views of the high mountains and glaciers make a fantastic backdrop for a picnic lunch. Children will enjoy paddling in the shallows and there are few more pleasant spots to relax with a baguette, some Bleu de Termignon cheese and a glass of Savoyard wine. The return route is a reversal of the outward route. It is mainly downhill and takes a little over an hour.

 ROUTE 2

La Pierre aux Pieds

Time	6hrs
Distance	13km
Ascent	1100m
Map	3633ET Haute Maurienne
Start	GR 0339 5018
Parking	Col de la Madeleine

A strange archaeological phenomenon high in a remote couloir, the Pierre aux Pieds are a set of footprints carved into a large slab of schist. Believed to date back to the Iron Age, their purpose remains a mystery. The route is easy to navigate, but it is quite a climb from the valley. The Refuge de Vallonbrun is a welcome stopping point for a coffee at least once, if not both on the way up and again on the way down!

Park at the lay-by marked 'Rocher d'Escalade de la Madeleine'. Follow the sign for the climbing venue but almost immediately take the narrow path off to the left (northwards) to gain the hamlet of le Collet. Locate the **chapel** opposite the path exit and take the GR5 to the left of the chapel. ▶ The GR5 climbs past the climbing venue of Dalles de Mollard and on to the ruins of the farm at le Mollard in about 1hr.

A sign for the refuge indicates about 30mins – this seems a very slow pace and 15–20mins is more realistic. On the way you pass the **chapel of St Antoine**, which is dedicated to mules and muleteers and the refuge is reached shortly after.

From the **refuge** ensure you don't miss the small rising path signed 'Pierre aux Pieds'. A few streams are crossed and again keep an eye out for a path signed off to the right (the route leaves the GR5 at this point). This path leads over a stream or two (no bridge this time) and around a shoulder. The path starts to steepen and then zigzags through some small outcrops before flattening off and all of a sudden the **Pierre aux Pieds** is there. The signs

This chapel is dedicated to St Madeleine, patron saint of prostitutes, perfumers and protector of harvests; quite a mix!

The Vallonbrun Refuge is a picturesque stop-off on the way to the Pierres aux Pieds

The mysterious footsteps carved into a rock high above the valley, the Pierres aux Pieds

clearly indicate no climbing on the rock and give a brief explanation in French as to its mysterious origins. From the refuge this climb will take around 1¾hrs.

The return is a reversal of the outward route; the refuge will be reached in about 1hr and the car park in 1hr or a little longer after that.

🚶 ROUTE 3
Lac Blanc and Plan des Eaux

Time	2½–3½hrs
Distance	6km
Ascent	300m
Map	3633ET Haute Maurienne
Start	GR 0330 5020
Parking	At le Coêtet – the car park is on the right at a sharp bend.

A short walk with a reasonable height gain and outstanding views into the main valley serves as a good first walk in the area. The walk as far as Lac Blanc is popular with occasional walkers, so the car park gets busy on sunny days.

See map p50.

The path leaves the road opposite the car park and climbs through some ruins, steadily gaining height as it wends its way to **Lac Blanc**. The views down into the valley are worthy of a few stops to locate familiar landmarks down below. It takes about 45mins walking for the unacclimatised to reach the lake side. As the path approaches the lake it becomes slightly indistinct and many little paths weave their way through the grass and rocks, but all paths lead to the shore. Following the path around the lake will allow you to look into the steep-sided gorge of the **Doron de Termignon** and may well turn your legs a little wobbly!

After exploring the lake and maybe partaking in a little sunbathing or fishing, take the signed path to the **Refuge du Lac Blanc**. The refuge is soon reached and the path becomes more of a vehicle track, making for easy walking. The refuge, as all refuges do, offers well-earned drinks and a range of meals and lighter snacks. The track continues to rise for about 1000m before descending to meet another vehicle track. Turn left and follow signage to Bellecombe. ▶ The track climbs to around 2380m before descending to join the road and passing a private chalet. The sharp turns can be short cut as the track descends.

On joining the road turn left and follow the road 100m to the car park at **Bellecombe**. At the car park cross the stream via a little wooden bridge and take the path bearing rightwards signed for le Coêtet. This path takes a reasonably straight line downhill. The views are superb and a few places offer themselves as picnic spots. Passing the tiny **Chapelle Ste Marguerite** (it's worth stopping for a peek inside), the path repeatedly crosses the road before joining it for the final descent to the car park. (Note: in

It is possible to take a short cut path directly onto this track a short distance before the junction.

Lac Blanc nestled among spectacular mountains

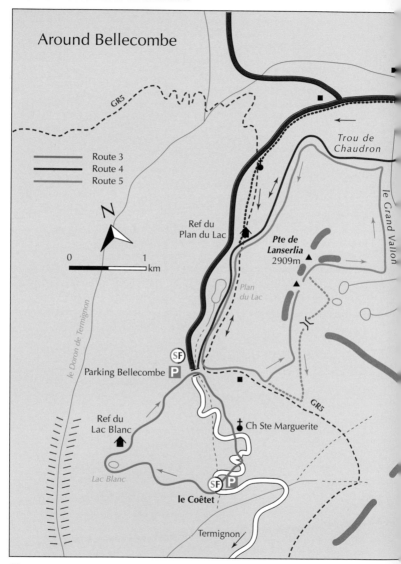

Around Bellecombe

Route 3
Route 4
Route 5

N

0   1
         km

Trou de
Chaudron

le Grand Vallon

GR5

Ref du
Plan du Lac

Pte de
Lanserlia
2909m

Plan
du Lac

SF
Parking Bellecombe P

le Doron de Termignon

Ref du
Lac Blanc

GR5

Ch Ste Marguerite

Lac Blanc

SF P

le Coêtet

Termignon

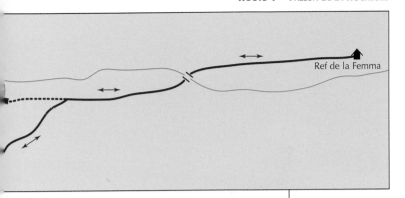

the final part of the descent the path does not follow the line indicated on the Top 25 map but drops much closer to the car park for a short road walk back uphill to the cars).

ROUTE 4

Vallon de la Rocheure

Time	5–6hrs
Distance	20km
Ascent	200m
Map	3633ET Haute Maurienne
Start	GR 0330 5022
Parking	Bellecombe car park (or take the shuttle bus, navette, from Termignon)

A long but pleasant walk at a reasonable altitude (around 2300m throughout) along a quiet valley, with no climbs of any note and a high likelihood of encountering marmots in the wild.

51

Refuge du Plan du Lac and la Grande Casse

Take the path from the car park, signposted Refuge de la Femma, beginning with a short rise alongside an impressive little canyon before levelling off for a pleasant walk past the small lake. The path contours right and gains a shoulder above the Refuge du Plan du Lac before continuing to contour into a small bowl, the Trou de Chaudron. Keep your eyes peeled for marmots; you'll probably hear their shrill warning whistles before spotting them among the rocks. After negotiating a short rockier (but horizontal) section the path descends to a track.

Bear right to follow the track up the valley, crossing a bridge before the track degenerates into a path. This path continues to the **refuge**, which stays hidden until you are quite close. The refuge has a colony of marmots living nearby; have a coffee or hot chocolate on the veranda, enjoy the view and see if you have sufficient patience to get good photographs of the comical creatures. When the author was last there he saw two French children creep up on a marmot; it saw them coming and disappeared into one of its holes. Very cleverly the girls took up an observation post above the hole and waited; equally cleverly the marmot popped out of another hole and sat observing the children. Who was watching who?

On this walk you are also likely to encounter the *pastou* which inhabit the valley. These large, white dogs protect the flocks of sheep that roam the mountainsides and need to be treated with respect. See the introduction for advice on how to behave in their presence.

To return to the car park retrace your steps or alternatively follow the track until it joins a tarmac road. Once here, catch the bus or follow the road uphill to **Chapelle St Barthélémy** then take the path on the left to **Refuge du Plan du Lac** (this is not a signposted path) before rejoining the path to **Bellecombe**. Ignore the 15mins indication – 25mins is more realistic.

ROUTE 5

Pointe de Lanserlia

Time	4–5hrs
Distance	6–10km
Ascent:	600m
Map	3633ET Haute Maurienne
Start	GR 0330 5022
Parking	Bellecombe (or take the shuttle bus from Termignon)

A straightforward ridge with far-reaching views is the climax of this walk. A reasonable starting height and short distance means you gain the 2900m contour without an enormous amount of ascent, not far from the magic 3000m contour.

Park at the Bellecombe car park and take the path signed Refuge du Cuchet, Refuge de Vallonbrun. Follow this fairly level track to the farm building **le Piou** (which sells eggs, cheese and butter should you wish to stock up for lunch). Shortly after the farm a small ravine crosses the track. Climb either side of this, straight up the hillside until a more level open combe is reached at around 2540m.

The simple summit ridge path of Pointe de Lanserlia

The skyline ridge on the left is the next objective; zigzag up to this and take time to enjoy the views down towards Termignon and Bramans. Keep to the ridge crest, which steadily improves its ridge-identity. The path also improves as height is gained. The cairn is reached at 2879m and the true ridge is now obvious, stretching towards the highest point in front. Follow the ridge down the slight descent to the col and climb towards the highest point, **Pointe de Lanserlia**. From here, the views are magnificent across to the Glaciers de Vanoise, Grande Casse and much of the valley to the Femma Refuge.

There are a number of options for a descent. The simplest is to retrace your steps to the col. Keep at least one eye on the path: the views in front are superb but the drop to the right is immense. Locate the path that climbs to the col from the little pools on the left. Descend towards the pools, skirting to the right to gain a small col. A path climbs from the track from earlier.

Probably the best circular route (and only about 1hr longer) is the descent via the eastern ridge and Grand Vallon. From the summit take the eastern ridge path (discernible on the ground but not very apparent all the time) into the **Grand Vallon** valley. Don't be tempted to cut the corner off when the obvious valley path becomes visible following the stream; if you do, you'll find yourself on reasonably steep grassy ground littered with boulders. Once the path is reached follow this down the secluded valley until you reach the high path near the Trou de Chaudron on the Femma Refuge path. Turn left and follow this over the scree and then on to the good path to the **Plan du Lac Refuge**. After a coffee (or lunch if you set off early) it is a short walk back to the car park.

ROUTE 6

Hannibal's Crossing (Col Clapier)

Time	5–6hrs
Distance	15km
Ascent	750m
Map	3634OT Val Cenis
Start:	GR 0331 5008
Parking:	Car park before Refuge du Suffet

This route follows what is thought by some to be the route Hannibal used to invade Italy (although no archaeological evidence of Hannibal's passing has ever been found on any of the passes or cols in the Alps). The only accounts of the journey are of Roman origin (and were written at least 100 years after the event) but they claim around 20,000 troops were lost crossing the pass in early winter. This route was used until the 16th century as a standard crossing into Italy. This will be a surprise as you walk the route, especially along the narrow paths through the forest. Today, the walk ought to take around 5–6hrs at most and proves no more taxing than a moderate mountain walk; to those earlier travellers it must have seemed a daunting prospect, especially in full skirts!

To access the start of the walk from Bramans, follow the minor road through the village and pass the Chapel St Pierre d'Extravache towards le Planey. Pick up the signage for the **Refuge du Suffet** and continue along the road until you come across a rough car park on the left. Park

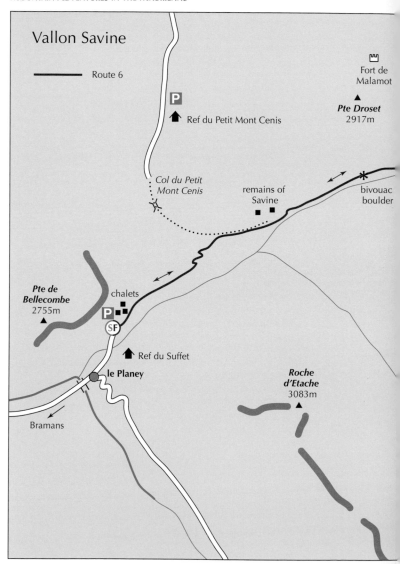

Vallon Savine

———— Route 6

P

⬆ Ref du Petit Mont Cenis

♜ Fort de Malamot

▲ **Pte Droset** 2917m

Col du Petit Mont Cenis

remains of Savine

✳ bivouac boulder

Pte de Bellecombe 2755m ▲

chalets

P SF

⬆ Ref du Suffet

● **le Planey**

Bramans

Roche d'Etache 3083m

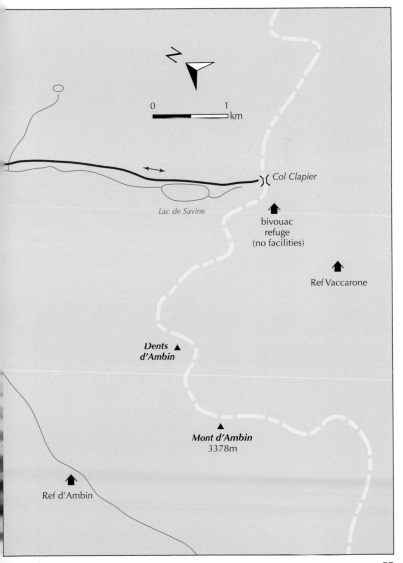

Col Clapier and Lac de Savine, said to be the site of Hannibal's camp and crossing to Italy

here and locate the sign explaining Hannibal's route (in French). Follow the signs up the zigzagging track, ignoring the level track off to the right, until a collection of three or four **chalets** is reached. Now follow the smaller path uphill into the trees. Signage at this point is for the Col de Petit Mont Cenis and sometimes Col Clapier or Lac de Savine.

The path climbs steadily upwards on a rising traverse before a number of zigzags and a sign off to the right onto a smaller path (which is not marked on the 1:25,000 map, but is on the 1:50,000). Take this path, which meets a track, and after a right turn you will soon pass a small wooden hut. Pass through a wooden gate on the track and follow the track downhill, then level, to reach the remains of the hamlet of Savine. The shrill whistle of marmots will no doubt echo through the valley here. Follow the obvious path up the wide valley, passing a huge boulder that could offer a bivouac site. The col ahead is not actually the Col Clapier; it is the headwall of glacial debris holding back the **Lac de Savine**. Roman accounts of the invasion of Italy say that Hannibal camped around here with 28,000 soldiers plus a baggage train and elephants. It is easy to imagine, as the area by the lake is a large, fairly flat plateau.

After 15mins **Col Clapier** and the Italian border are reached. Built into the rock at the summit is the remains of a frontier post (this area has been hotly contested for centuries). According to Pliny, on gaining the col Hannibal stood atop a large rock and looked down into Italy – now it is your turn. A refuge below has no resident guardian and is more like a bothy than the refuges you may be used to – no coffee here unless you bring your own!

It would be possible to descend into Italy as far as Susa and return by bus, although this would be a long day and a huge descent – over 1500m. A simple return via the route taken up is more in keeping with a short day walk.

Note: a shorter day could be had by starting at the Refuge du Petit Mont Cenis but would miss following the valley from Bramans. It would also be possible to cycle in from the Refuge du Petit Mont Cenis, a round trip of 3 to 4hrs or so.

 ROUTE 7

Mont Froid

Time	3–6½ hours depending on route choices
Distance	9–13km
Ascent	750m
Map	3634OT Val Cenis
Start	GR 0324 5010
Parking	Refuge du Petit Mont Cenis

A reasonably short walk out but one with fine views and some historical interest. The remains of the fort on the summit ridge make for an interesting exploration and the barracks blocks were occupied until comparatively regent times. In winter this area is still used by the French army as a training ground, with troops skiing in and out of the areas to develop survival skills and off-piste skiing. This walk and Route 8 to Pointe de Bellecombe can be combined for a more challenging full day out. A popular walk, so solitude is unlikely!

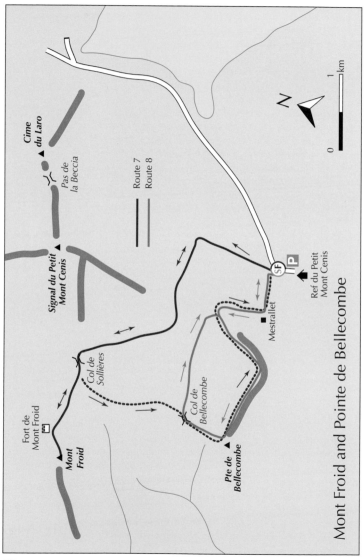

Mont Froid and Pointe de Bellecombe

Remains of fortifications on the summit of Mont Froid dating back to Napoleonic times

Park at the rough and stony car park near the Refuge du Petit Mont Cenis and then walk back up the road to the signpost 'Col de Sollières, Mont Froid 2hrs'. Follow this path through open ground carpeted with wild flowers; keep an eye out for eagles and vultures hunting on the slopes above. The path passes through a white rock band that resembles old mining waste to gain the **Col de Sollières** in about 1¼hrs or a little more. The path to **Mont Froid** is signed here and is obvious on the hillside above. The **fort** remains are gained after about 15–20mins; the true summit (2822m) lies about 10 easy minutes further along the path. ▸ A fabulous view across the Maurienne valley to the glaciers is a just reward for the climb and now is probably a good time to stop and have lunch while soaking in the views.

The war memorial here is identical to others on nearby summits and reflects the bravery and losses on both sides in April 1945.

There are several options for the return route. The shortest involves retracing your steps or, for a longer route, follow the Peace Way from the Col de Sollières to **Col de Bellecombe** then return to the car park. A further option is to follow the Peace Way to Col de Bellecombe, climb **Pointe de Bellecombe** and follow its ridgeline before regaining the path by **Mestrallet** farmstead and returning to the car park. This would equate to a day of a good 6hrs or more in all and around 1000m of ascent.

Be aware that the Peace Way is not a well-used path yet and tends to fade out on the ground in places; take care as the more obvious path descends to Col des Archettes while the Peace Way bears left in a southerly direction. The Peace Way waymarking here is a series of small yellow posts and small painted white squares with blue stars, both of which tend to blend into the wild flowers. At Col de Bellecombe there is a signpost, but the col itself is not as apparent as may be expected.

ROUTE 8

Pointe de Bellecombe

Time	4–4½hrs
Distance	9km
Ascent	750m
Map	3634OT Val Cenis
Start	GR 0324 5010
Parking:	Refuge du Petit Mont Cenis

Pointe de Bellecombe looks desperately boring from one side but from the other it is an incredibly dramatic ridgeline with an enormous drop of over 1000m to the le Planey valley far below. It is easy to imagine local tribesmen levering rocks onto Hannibal and his men as they travelled through the valley beneath your feet! This walk can be combined with Route 7 for a longer day.

From the refuge car park walk back to the road junction and take the Mont Froid/Col de Sollières path, but after around 200m take the path bearing left flanking the hillside. The large and quite impressive cliffs ahead form the boundary to the beginning of the ridgewalk later. The path crosses the stream 200–300m above the farmstead of **Mestrallet**. Having crossed the stream, follow the path up the western bank and continue left around a broad shoulder into a large combe.

The path may become indistinct at times and the white squares that are the signage are difficult to spot, but the general route is fairly apparent. Once in the combe the path keeps to the left-hand side – a largish stream and gully will be on the right. Continue gaining height as you make your way to the low point on the skyline. Once on the ridgeline, simply follow it right and enjoy the increasing exposure. Should anyone not appreciate the dizzying heights, it is very easy to follow the line of the ridge a safe distance away. At every step the views improve as you peek into the abyss below. A number of bastions may tempt you into some airy exploration and photographs, but take care as some of the rock is quite loose. The summit of **Pointe de Bellecombe** arrives all too soon if you're

Summit of Pointe de Bellecombe with the considerable exposure and ridge evident

A memorial plaque at
the summit reminds
you of the most
recent conflict here
during April 1945.

enjoying the views, not soon enough if your calves are
burning! ◀ The views from here are fabulous and many
other summits are visible, including Roche d'Etache,
the right-hand skyline of which forms one of the mountaineering routes; much of Hannibal's Crossing and the
Signal du Petit Mont Cenis are also clearly visible.

There are a number of options from the summit.
A reversal of the route will appeal to those who enjoy
the exposure. Alternatively, a steep but straightforward
descent to Col de Bellecombe then allows two further
options: one is to return down to the combe and retrace
your steps; another is to follow the vague path to Col de
Sollières and Mont Froid to gain another summit and
explore the fort on the summit. To return to the car follow the well-trodden path from the Col de Sollières to the
Refuge du Petit Mont Cenis. This is clearly marked and
takes approximately 1hr.

ROUTE 9

High Valley Walk

Time	6–7hrs
Distance	15km
Ascent	800m
Map	3633ET Haute Maurienne
Start	GR 0330 5020
Parking	Termignon village

A mixture of forest-shaded paths and open high pasture make this a pleasant
walk. Surprises abound – gun emplacements from World War II litter a
plateau above Termignon; you join the famous GR5 and there is enough
ascent to have climbed almost any Lakeland peak yet the valley sides still
soar above. Views down and across the valley abound and serve as a good
viewpoint for two of the mountaineering ridge routes.

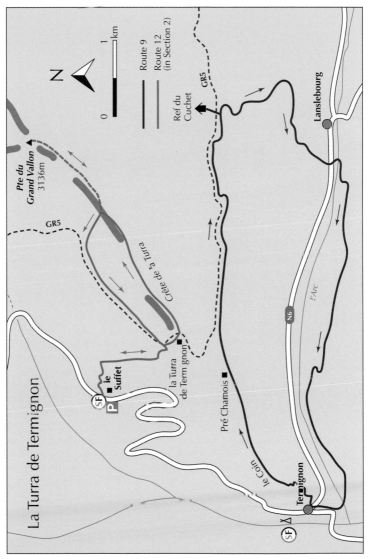

An almost aerial view of Termignon from the path leading to le Coin

Start from the village of Termignon, or park in the lay-by just before the hairpin corner on the up-valley road out of Termignon (this will mean an unwelcome uphill finish to the walk). Having walked round the hairpin take the footpath on the left into the wood. Steadily gain height through the trees, passing a pylon, and continue to a transmitter mast. At **le Coin** (remains of buildings can be seen amongst the trees) there is a short level section. You will be able to locate gunnery platforms along this section dating back to World War II. It is hard to imagine French forces shelling the invasion forces in the valley below.

The path continues to climb, and at a junction of paths take the path signposted for Pré Chamois. Eventually the path joins the GR5, which presents itself as a track; turn right for a welcome descent. This soon turns into another climb and the views open out onto the valley far below. The route enters high pasture ground and passes some summer chalets. Either climb to the **Refuge du Cuchet** (often unstaffed) or turn right to follow the path down towards **Lanslebourg**. This path grows into a track as you descend and eventually enters the village. Take the road (Rue de la Ramasse) between La Chèvrerie 'Chez Jo' and the Auberge Do-Re to the bridge and follow the Chemin du Petit Bonheur back to Termignon. This track is easy to follow and climbs gently for the first third before beginning a descent past the ski lift and new buildings into **Termignon**.

ROUTE 10

Pointe de l'Observatoire

Time	7hrs
Distance	13km
Ascent	1000m
Map	3534OT Trois Vallées
Start	GR 0321 5014
Parking	Car park at the dam wall, Plan d'Amont

The 3000m contour is crossed and the scenery turns decidedly rocky on this walk. Although this walk can be done in a day, it can be turned into a first-time Alpine expedition by booking a night in the Refuge du Fond d'Aussois. Be sure to phone and book before setting out.

From the car park at the **upper dam** follow the track gaining height above the dam, past an information board, and cross a bridge beyond the waterfall feeding into the reservoir. A path leaves the track here and more or less follows the stream to begin with before veering right and rejoining the main path. The signage indicates following the main path to the right, which then doubles back on itself and continues up the valley, the path previously mentioned joins this main path and continues towards the refuge. Pass a very small chapel and the old refuge. After 1–1½hrs you will reach a modern-looking refuge,

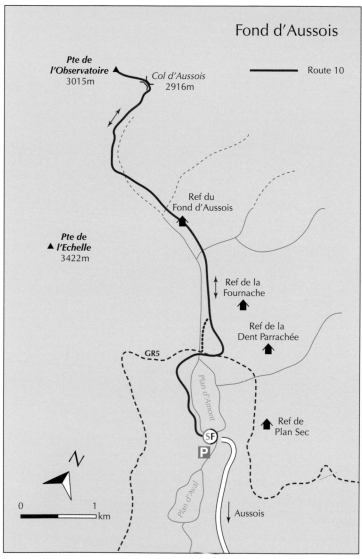

Fond d'Aussois

━━━━ Route 10

Pte de l'Observatoire 3015m

Col d'Aussois 2916m

Ref du Fond d'Aussois

Pte de l'Echelle ▲ 3422m

Ref de la Fournache

Ref de la Dent Parrachée

GR5

Plan d'Amont

Ref de Plan Sec

SF

P

Plan d'Aval

Aussois

0   1 km

Refuge du Fond d'Aussois, that would not look out of place in a design competition.

Continue up the valley on a good path that begins the climb up to Col d'Aussois in earnest. Cairns help to distinguish the path as the ground gets rockier; a white cross will become visible on the skyline. ▶ Near the white cross the ground levels off onto a small plateau; the path bears right and the **Pointe de l'Observatoire** is apparent on the left. A short final climb will see you sitting on the summit with significant exposure on one side. There are a number of rock climbs up this face; it goes without saying that anything dropped could have fatal consequences for those below.

To descend reverse the route.

This does not mark the col but is set a few hundred metres before it.

The Pointe de l'Observatoire is dwarfed by the enormous Pointe de l'Echelle.

2 MOUNTAINEERING ROUTES

The real peaks of the mountains are hard won. They usually involve significant ascent and considerable exposure, and require confidence and a range of technical skills. These routes have the potential to be both the most rewarding and the most dangerous in this book. Scrambling often involves moving un-roped in exposed situations and you need to be certain you have the necessary skills and experience to take these routes on. Confidence in moving on rock which may be loose and, even in August, have a light snow covering is essential. The skills to use a rope effectively to protect the party are a pre-requisite on some routes. A minimum recommendation is a 35m rope, and one or two slings and karabiners per person. The Alpine style of moving together roped up is very effective on ridges, as long as you can manage the rope correctly. Learn these skills prior to attempting any of these routes!

The grades given are the author's impressions: climbers may find them over cautious; walkers may find them more challenging. To enjoy these routes you should have some classic UK ridges under your belt (Crib Goch, Sharp Edge, CMD Arête, Pinnacle Ridge on St Sunday Crag are not dissimilar to these routes) and be

The airy but simple summit of Petit Vallon with Mont d'Ambin and Col d'Agne behind (Route 16)

'The summit's that way!' Pointe Fournache summit is only a waypoint on the route to Dent Parrachée. Mont Banc is visible in the background (Route 22)

acclimatised, as many of them are at an altitude of more than 3000m.

Equipment

Experienced scramblers might not get a rope out of their sack for any of these routes. Less confident groups should rope up and move either in unison, using the correct techniques to ensure everyone on the rope is safe at all times, or tackle the more difficult sections pitched and belayed accordingly. The times given are for competent parties without a rope in good conditions; add at least an hour or two for pitching the routes. Even experienced scramblers will carry a rope on routes of this nature; you never know when it could help you out of a tricky situation.

As a bare minimum for scrambling carry:

- 35m of single rope – a 9mm rope is suitable for these routes
- 2 slings and karabiners each
- stiff boots – there are plenty of light, stiff boots designed for this type of route

You should also know how to belay with an Italian hitch.

Scramblers enjoy the freedom of moving unencumbered across ridges and slabs; this freedom comes at a cost – of not having the added security offered by belays, harnesses, and runners. Please bear this in mind and remember Whymper's advice: 'Do nothing in haste; look well to each step; and from the beginning think what may be the end.'

The schist rock on most of these routes is rough and provides great friction in the dry; in the wet, or with a scattering of snow, it can be slippery and unpleasant. Save these routes for a sunny day and relish the views that go with the clear weather. The ridges have a multitude of natural pinnacles to provide belays and running belays. Also remember that these routes are less busy than many UK routes and are subjected to much more vigorous weathering, meaning loose blocks and unstable scree are part of the mountain environment.

ROUTE 11
Pointe Droset

Time	5–6hrs
Distance	12km
Ascent	800m
Map	3634OT Val Cenis
Start	GR 0335 5011
Parking	Chapelle St Barthélémy
Grade	-1

More of a rough walk than a scramble, this route reaches a fortified summit via an easy ridge where every difficulty can be bypassed or taken head on at will. The extensive fort remains at the summit make for an interesting exploration.

From the Col du Mont Cenis the road is signposted to the Refuge du Petit Mont Cenis. This road is rough in places but perfectly driveable. Follow the road until reaching the small Chapelle St Barthélémy and park here where the road splits with the left-hand road leading following the lake.

Walk along the road towards the refuge. Before the refuge is reached there is a large stony car park with a track leading left towards some power lines. This old track climbs gently towards a water management building and onwards to around 2300m where a short and steep path cuts off a long loop of the track. This levels off at the spot height of 2467m and the ridge is clearly visible on the right.

Ascend to the base of the ridge. The ridge is straightforward, with plenty of opportunity to bypass any difficulties. After passing a few cantilever stones, a gently angled slab can be tackled – the descent off this is more challenging than the ascent. The ridge continues, with options and opt-outs available throughout. A couple of false summits give way to the actual summit of **Pointe**

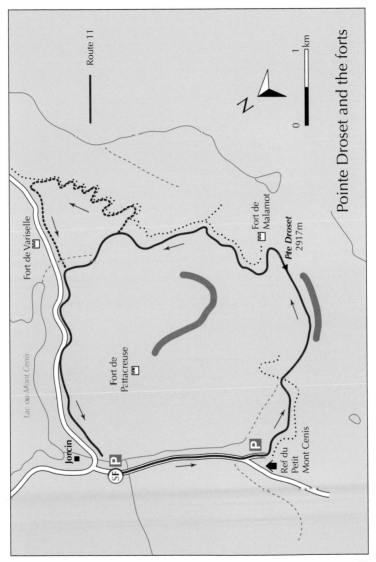

Pointe Droset and the forts

— Route 11

N

0 ————— 1 km

Fort de Variselle

Lac ou Mont Cenis

Jorcin

SF P

Fort de Pettacreuse

Fort de Malamot

Pte Droset 2917m

P

Ref du Petit Mont Cenis

Droset (2917m), which has a number of cairns on its broad top. The views down into the Savine valley and towards Col Clapier along the ridge are fabulous, as is the view across to the Dents d'Ambin.

The long whaleback summit leads to the remains of **Fort de Malamot** and a number of gun emplacements worthy of exploration. A headtorch will make this much more fruitful. From the fort, a good military track leads down, doubling back on itself and passing heaps of abandoned barbed wire from the fortifications. Still more gun emplacements litter the mountainside, but start to give way to vegetation and edelweiss growing amongst the stones. The track descends quite steeply at times to reach a sort of T junction. Take the left-hand track here and follow this military road all the way to the lake road. Alternatively take a narrower path which leaves the track near some buildings at approximately 2580m. This path is indistinct at times, but keep to the left of a dry stream bed to join the lake road and turn left to return to the start.

A subterranean camouflaged gun port built into the summit of Pointe Droset. Take a headtorch to explore the complex more fully

ROUTE 12
Crête de la Turra and Pointe du Grand Vallon

Time	6–7½hrs
Distance	11km
Ascent	1280m
Map	3633ET Haute Maurienne
Start	GR 0330 5019
Parking	Le Suffet
Grade	1

La Turra de Termignon dominates the village of Termignon and certainly looks impressive, but fails to live up to its image as you ascend it and discover it is really a plateau. Luckily, it also serves as the start to an interesting ridgeline scramble, with opt-out options throughout.

The route begins at le Suffet on the road to Bellecombe; there is off road parking for about 10 cars on the left. From the car park, walk up the road for about 20m and take a farm track on the right, which is signed as a private road closed to cars. Follow this path which trends left almost immediately. A number of zigzags follow; keep taking the main track each time you encounter a junction of paths.

After passing some ruined farm buildings close to the treeline the track starts levelling out to gain the shoulder of **la Turra de Termignon** in about 1–1½ hrs. Two or three farm buildings are visible. Beware the path here is slightly confusing: take the path to the left of the farm buildings, which becomes indistinct, but some faint blue, white and red painted signing helps. The path gains and keeps close to the ridgeline above the farm buildings, allowing enjoyable scrambling which can be avoided at will, making it great for novices. Some blocks can be quite a challenge if you want to up the ante.

At spot height 2794m, a slight descent follows and marks the end of the scrambling. The ground levels off, and at a point around 2850m locate scree on the left. Descend this scree to gain the GR5 with care. There are a few small drop-offs to be aware of so, as always, take care in descent. Turn left along the GR5 (at this point it is little more than a narrow path) until it joins a larger farm track at 2283m. Veer downhill to regain the track from this morning which returns to le Suffet.

Another option could be to reverse the route from the high point of 2794m to maximise the scrambling adding about an hour to the time.

A challenging extension is to continue from the descent point along the ridge to gain the **Pointe du Grand Vallon** (3136m) and break the 10,000ft contour; this will

add another hour or so to the route. The views from here are far reaching and well worth the effort as they are so extensive – the whole of the ski domain is visible and many other routes in this book can be identified from this summit.

Passing the first rock pinnacles above the Turra plateau

ROUTE 13

Pointe des Fours

Time	4–5hrs
Distance	6km
Ascent	550m
Map	3633ET Haute Maurienne
Start	GR 0346 5030
Parking	Pont de la Neige, Col de l'Iseran
Grade	1

A short route starting from over 2500m means gaining the 3000m mark is relatively painless. Straightforward scrambling along a ridge can be escaped at any time, allowing a mixed ability party to enjoy an adventurous challenge.

Starting from Pont de la Neige on the road to Col de l'Iseran means you have 'climbed' around 800m from the valley already! As you cross the bridge, there is a small car park on the left and a path signposted 'Col des Fours, 1hr 50 min' – this is the approach path. It follows the right bank of the stream, then picks a way over rougher, looser ground. Gain the false col with the remains of a glacier on the right (little more than a permanent snow field today).

Once the false col is gained, the path to the real col is visible on the right. The traverse soon leads to the col with a cairn atop. This holds a sort of letterbox, where you may find an addressed and stamped postcard left by a previous visitor. If so, take it with you, adding a short note, and pop it in a post box in the valley. The obvious ridge to the summit is on the left as **Col des Fours** is reached. A vague path below the ridge exists as an escape or poor weather option.

Delightful scrambling on the pinnacled ridge to Pointe des Fours

The ridge is a good grade 1 scramble in the dry. In the wet or light snow the rock is very slippery and encourages a slip to the right, as it all dips in that direction.

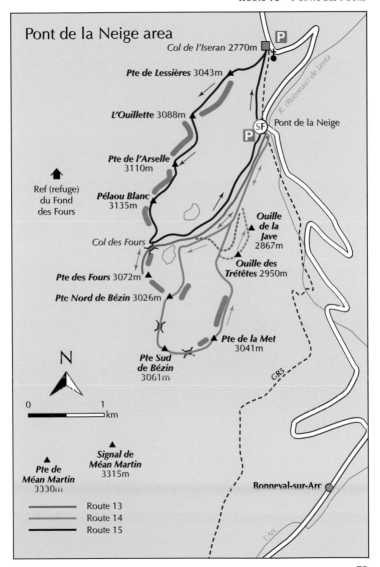

Pont de la Neige area

Col de l'Iseran 2770m

Pte de Lessières 3043m

L'Ouillette 3088m

Pte de l'Arselle 3110m

Pélaou Blanc 3135m

Ref (refuge) du Fond des Fours

Col des Fours

Pte des Fours 3072m

Pte Nord de Bézin 3026m

Pte Sud de Bézin 3061m

Pte de la Met 3041m

Ouille de la Jave 2867m

Ouille des Trétêtes 2950m

R. (Ruisseau) de Lenta

Pont de la Neige

N

0   1 km

Pte de Méan Martin 3330m

Signal de Méan Martin 3315m

GR5

Bonneval-sur-Arc

l'Arc

Route 13
Route 14
Route 15

A fall to the left would be very unwelcome as the drop is both very steep and very rough! After 40mins to 1hr the summit of **Pointe des Fours** (3072m) is gained and with it a fabulous panorama, including Mont Blanc in the distance. Reverse your route to the false col and then take your pick of descending via Ouille des Trétêtes and Ouille de la Jave for a technical ridgewalk or returning the way you came.

ROUTE 14
3000ers Circuit

Time	4–5hrs
Distance	8km
Ascent	800m
Map	3633ET Haute Maurienne
Start	GR 0346 5030
Parking	Pont de la Neige, Col de l'Iseran
Grade	1, short section of exposed 2+

The Pont de la Neige gives easy access to a lot of 3000m summits without a long approach. This option allows at least four summits to be reached on quite a short day. The scrambling is mainly straightforward, but one short section is much more challenging.

Follow the path towards **Col des Fours** from the car park as described in Route 13. On reaching the false col pass the lake south of the col on its eastern side and gain the ridgeline to the left of the summit, Pointe Nord de Bézin. The scramble along the ridge to the first summit block is quite loose in places, so take care. The descent from this summit block is quite tricky and a rope is advised for all but the most experienced scramblers, as a fall would be serious. This is a short section, no more than 20 or 30m, before easier scrambling ground is reached. Follow

the ridge to reach **Pointe Nord de Bézin** at 3026m; a descent southwards on scree follows before traversing rough ground to the Col du Bézin. Alternatively, the Pointe Nord de Bézin ridge and summit can be avoided by continuing to the right under the summit and gaining the col between Pointe des Fours and Pointe Nord de Bézin. ▶ This makes the circuit substantially easier but does miss out the real challenge of the day and makes this a rough walk rather than scramble.

From the col, a good path to **Pointe Sud de Bézin** is followed to the summit at 3061m – there are great views from here. A short descent follows towards **Pointe de la Met** and another short climb reaches its summit (3041m). The northerly ridge to the Ruisseau des Fonds is delightful. From here, the climb to the col between **Ouille des Trétêtes** and the 2947m summit of le Grand Fond is not very long, and then a short descent to the path taken earlier this morning (unless you fancy grabbing yet more summits by taking the ridge over Ouille des Trétêtes and Ouille de la Jave) takes you back to the car park.

Pointe Nord de Bézin, the difficult descent section is clearly visible as a notch on the skyline.

Older printed maps indicate a glacier here but global warming has disposed of it all.

81

ROUTE 15

Lessières Traverse

Time	5hrs
Distance	8km
Ascent	750m
Map	3633ET Haute Maurienne
Start	GR 0346 5031
Parking	Col de l'Iseran
Grade	PD

This traverse is reminiscent of the Aonach Eagach ridge; it has a lot of airy scrambling following an obvious ridgeline that never disappoints. The route covers four summits, all over 3000m, with a surprisingly small amount of ascent owing to the start point at the summit of the highest road col in Europe. Some sections are quite exposed with few alternatives but the rock has good friction and slopes to provide reassuring incut handholds on the left side of the route. The other side offers less positive holds as they tend to slope awkwardly but is less exposed. The schist along this route has very good friction qualities in the dry, but is slippery and unnerving in the wet and best avoided after a period of rain.

From the Col de l'Iseran car park and restaurant take the clear path that is to the right of the church and signposted – this quickly gains the ridge. Follow this path to gain the summit of **Pointe des Lessières**. There is a short section of cabling at one point, although this section is straightforward and the cable serves to aid adventurous sightseers from the col. ◀

From the summit, it is possible to see the whole of the ridge stretching out ahead to Pélaou Blanc.

A short section of downclimbing from the summit allows easier access along the ridge; this is probably one of the more challenging sections. The ridge to **l'Ouillette** is pleasantly enjoyable, offering a few short challenges but generally easier ground. A path on the right-hand side of the ridge offers a less exposed route, if preferred.

Continue along the ridge to **Pointe de l'Arselle** on rough rock following the crest or the less exposed path; after the Pointe, the route descends to the Col de l'Arcelle where an escape route to the left descending on scree is possible. The ridge continues to **Pélaou Blanc**, the highest point of the day at 3135m.

The Lessières ridge invitingly stretches into the distance. With only about 300m ascent to the start of this magnificent traverse it is a must-do

The descent from the summit involves some simple downclimbing, and a vague path steadily improves as it reaches **Col des Fours**, with Pointe des Fours behind it. This summit could be climbed following the description in Route 13 if time, and energy, permits. The descent from the col is a simple walk following the path left from the col and descending to **Pont de la Neige**. From here, hitch-hiking back to the start point is an option, but the walk back takes less than an hour and follows the unmarked but clear narrow path which climbs on the grassy hillside above the road to gain the **Col de l'Iseran**.

A fit and acclimatised party could do a 'there and back' route along the ridge for a truly memorable day, or do the route in reverse starting at Pont de la Neige – this would involve more ascent, but would allow a welcome tea stop at the restaurant before the descent back to the car.

ROUTE 16

Le Petit Vallon

Time	6–7hrs
Distance	13km
Ascent	1100m
Map	3634OT Val Cenis
Start	GR 0329 5006
Parking	Chalets de St Barthélémy
Grade:	-1

The expansive views from the summit and the lunar-like upper reaches of the Petit Vallon are likely to be enjoyed in solitude on this long and challenging walk. The technical sections are short and straightforward although hands will be needed on a few sections.

From the small car park at Chalets de St Barthélémy, take the obvious track that passes the few chalets (real farm chalets, not holiday venues) selling cheese and eggs. The tiny chapel hidden in the rock outcrop should not be missed – an incredible structure perfectly camouflaged.

The track continues to a track junction. The path to the right leads down to a wooden bridge crossing the river – this forms part of the return route. For now, take the signed track to 'Pas de la Coche par le sentier des glaces (passage délicats)'. This path climbs steadily as it follows the riverside; some old snow patches may well be encountered into August, but are easily crossed – a trekking pole is all that is required. The path climbs more steeply and hands may be required in a few spots to overcome some short, steep steps. A flat area is reached after this challenging section and after a short distance across the plateau, the waymarked path is encountered – red and yellow markings indicate the way across glacier-worn rocks. The markings can be difficult spot at times,

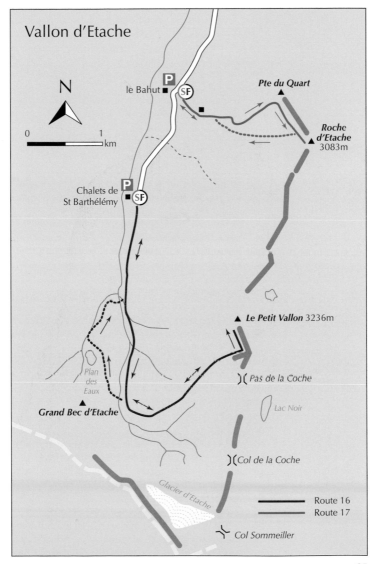

Vallon d'Etache

N

0   1
km

le Bahut ■ P SF

Pte du Quart ▲

Roche
d'Etache
3083m ▲

Chalets de
St Barthélémy ■ P SF

▲ Le Petit Vallon 3236m

)(Pas de la Coche

Lac Noir

Plan
des
Eaux

Grand Bec d'Etache ▲

)(Col de la Coche

Glacier d'Etache

——— Route 16
——— Route 17

⤚ Col Sommeiller

The path towards Fond d'Etache with the impressive Grand Bec d'Etache towering over the valley

but the path generally follows the streambed towards a small lake, which is passed to its left.

Keep an eye on the skyline to locate a scree run leading to a col marked 3085m on the map and the ridge leading to the summit of **Le Petit Vallon** (3236m). Do not be tempted by the faint line leading through the scree to this col – the ground is loose and steep in places. It is much better to continue around on a more level route (albeit unmarked and mainly untrodden) to cross the Ruisseau de Plan d'Etache. The base of the green tongue of grassy ground leads to an easier route on more stable terrain to the col. From the col, the view across to the Ambin range is spectacular – the Val d'Ambin, the Mont d'Ambin and Dents d'Ambin are all impressive. The ridge leads north to a final mini couloir, which gains a level summit ridge to a fabulous view point on the summit. Mont Blanc, la Dent Parrachée, the Italian Piedmont and the Glaciers de la Vanoise are all laid out. ◄

To fully appreciate the view binoculars are a must.

The descent begins with retracing your steps, but beware not to follow the summit ridge too far as it leads onto the east ridge; descend to the col and back down to the Ruisseau de Plan d'Etache. The descent past the lake is pleasant and relaxing and the rock hopping on the river bed very enjoyable. To vary the return, it is possible to continue along the path, following signs for Plan des Eaux. The small tarn here makes for a relaxing stop before descending to cross the river at a wooden bridge, and the path returns to the chalets.

 ROUTE 17
Roche d'Etache

Time	4–5hrs
Distance	7km
Ascent	1135m
Map	3634OT Val Cenis
Start	GR 0330 5007
Parking	le Bahut, end of metalled road to St Barthélémy
Grade:	1+

A steep ascent to gain a rocky ridge is rewarded by a scramble peppered with rock pinnacles; difficulties can be by-passed, and from the summit you can trace the route Hannibal is supposed to have used to cross the Alps through the valley below.

The route starts from a point at which the metalled road becomes a dirt track. There is no parking as such: you need to pull off the road, bearing in mind that the road/track is used by people driving further up the valley to the car park at St Barthélémy. On the 1:25,000 map this is marked as le Bahut but there are no signs for this; the chalet/farm buildings have a sign, Les Mélèzes. The track from the road is an obvious dirt farm track; take the left split of the track and continue to gain height. At the upper barns and farm buildings, follow the path to the right behind the hut close to the stream. This climbs quite

Roche d'Etache: the route follows the right-hand ridge

steeply and is narrow, becoming indistinct in places. Another path leads off left from these buildings; this seems good to start with but becomes more indistinct as height is gained.

After what seems a long ascent a large, open-mouthed cwm is reached. Take a breather here and admire the view! The ridge forms the skyline in front; take time to identify a green tongue of vegetation penetrating the looser, rocky ground to the left. The left path option brings you to the combe closer to this green tongue; the right path will have you close to a moraine. Either way, you need to ascend the tongue and reach the col to the right of **Pointe du Quart**.

Scrambling starts at the col and follows the ridgeline. At around 2800m it is necessary to traverse to the right under a cliff barring the way. It is usually best to choose a path to the right side for any obstacles encountered along the ridge: left seems very exposed. The views get better and better all the time and the summit of **Roche d'Etache** arrives as something of a surprise. This ridgeline carries on for what looks like miles and seems to try to entice you to go on to the next peak, and the next, and the next... This is a long enough day without adding to it, but the thought of a Cuillin-like traverse will drift into the minds of those with bigger ambitions.

There are two options now for descent. Reversing the route in its entirety is one option. Another is to follow the ridge back for a short while before turning into the cwm for some boulder and scree hopping. Do not be tempted into running the scree, as there are a number of small cliffs that are almost invisible from above. A steady pace is best and safest. The ground gets better the further you descend and a number of paths weave in and out, appearing and disappearing as they go. Aim towards the moraine you can see (the same one you saw in the morning if you came up on the right-hand track), pick up the path and follow it steeply down to the farm buildings and then on down to the road. Most of the day is spent on rough rock and your boots will be showing signs of this by the end of the day!

ROUTE 18
Traverse of Pointe de Cugne

Time	4–5hrs
Distance	8km
Ascent	910m
Map	3634OT Val Cenis
Start	GR 0321 5015
Parking	Termignon village
Grade	1+

This traverse of Pointe de Cugne makes a great outing on Tuesdays, when the chair lifts from Termignon run to Replat des Canons. This substantially reduces the long walk in and out. In 2009 the return lift cost €6. Without the chair lift, you'll need to add 800m ascent and 8km of walking from Termignon, or around 2–3hrs and about 4km from the fromagerie at la Ramasse – a mountain bike could be used for this approach. This route description assumes you have taken the chair lifts to the wonderful revolving café at the Replat des Canons.

Note Make sure you do not miss the last lift down. (Times may vary – check before you set off.) An early start pays dividends.

From the café, take the path signed 'l'Erellaz' and follow this for two bends before taking a narrower path on the left (look out for the red-painted marker). This is a steeper but much shorter path through the trees. A sign 'Pte de

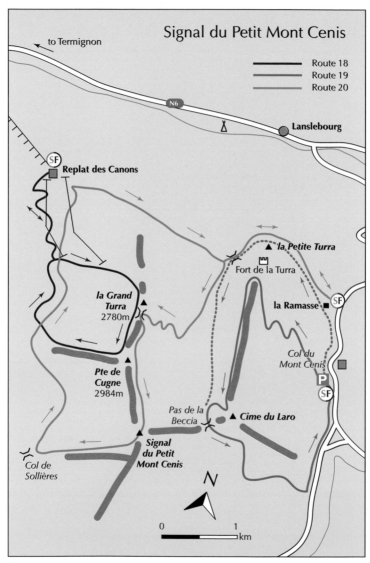

Signal du Petit Mont Cenis

Route 18
Route 19
Route 20

to Termignon

N6

Lanslebourg

SF

Replat des Canons

la Petite Turra

Fort de la Turra

la Ramasse

SF

la Grand Turra
2780m

Pte de Cugne
2984m

Col du Mont Cenis

P

SF

Pas de la Beccia

Cime du Laro

Col de Sollières

Signal du Petit Mont Cenis

N

0   1
km

Cugne 2h 30mins, Sig du Mt Cenis 3h 30mins' indicates the direction; the waymarking of this path is not wonderful but the ski lift pylons are more than enough of a waymarker. An hour of walking from the café brings you to the top of the drag lift; there is a vague path leading off to the skyline ridge and telecom mast – this is the first waypoint for the route. Take a moment to admire the view and locate the route along the skyline visible in front.

After a steady climb you reach the mast and the real fun begins! The ground from the mast to the summit of **la Grand Turra** (2780m) is easy enough, but changes to predominantly rocky terrain. A short but slightly awkward descent to the Col de Randouillards follows, and then the thoroughly enjoyable ridge begins. An hour of pure scrambling on rough, good rock along the ridge to the summit of **Pointe de Cugne** (2984m) follows. A better lunch stop will be hard to find!

The descent ridge runs west from the summit and is much easier than the ascent. There are numerous opportunities for exposure for those who want it, but all can be avoided too. A particularly attractive section marks the

The descent ridge is as enjoyable as the ascent and could offer an easier way up for novices

end of any challenges and the ridge surrenders to simple grass slopes and loose rock. Pick a route to the right to regain the farm track visible below. This track leads back to the café, with plenty of options to cut corners or take ski runs directly down (these are inevitably very steep and unrelenting). Enjoy a well-earned drink at the café before taking the chair lift down.

 ROUTE 19

North Ridge of Cime du Laro

Time	4–7hrs
Distance	10km
Ascent	800m
Map	3634OT Val Cenis
Start	GR 0335 5014
Parking	Col du Mont Cenis
Grade:	1+

This is a fabulous route along an ever more interesting ridge. Photo opportunities galore and great views all around combine to make this a great day. Remnants of old frontlines will amaze you, and leave you wondering how you can wage a war on such mountainsides. A convenient military hut can serve as a rendezvous for members of the party not wishing to follow the ridge.

Park at the car park opposite the bar and café. It is hard to imagine that in winter the bar is completely snowed in and tables and chairs are set out on what is the road in summer. Skidoos are the only mechanised transport here, and most people arrive on snow shoes or skis. Take the obvious signed path towards the old fort, **Fort de la Turra**, visible on the skyline. The first target for the day is the col to the left of the fort. Steady climbing will see the col reached in around 1hr. Unless you plan to investigate

The first pinnacles on the north ridge of Cime du Laro offer good friction and a spectacular situation

the fort (a popular day trip in itself), turn left and keep close to the ridgeline. An old *cabane* is soon discovered – quite a lonely look-out post during the war. The views across the Lac du Mont Cenis and along the valley are breathtaking. Close by is a marker stone of the Italian–French border from 1930, the first indication of long-running border disputes along this ridgeline. This must be a contender for the most picturesque frontline. Some old dugouts and barbed wire are encountered as the ridge continues; it steepens all the time and becomes rockier as height is gained.

The first serious piece of scrambling comes as something of a surprise. A steep bastion looms and at first sight seems impassable. A simple bypass to the right overcomes this difficulty and the ridge starts to show itself in its rocky splendour. An altimeter will inform you that there isn't much more height to be gained, but what there is as good as anything on Striding Edge. A final bastion seems impassable, but by following an indistinct path to the left easier ground is soon reached. A short gully bars the way, but follow this and the summit will be

The troop shelter near the Pas de la Beccia

waiting – with a sting in its tail. A very narrow defile separates you from the true summit. Cross carefully to gain **Cime du Laro** (2881m).

The descent gully is to the right of this defile and needs to be treated with care and respect – take care not to dislodge any rocks or stones. Look out for a levelled piece of ground to the left at about a third of the way down – yet more wartime remains can be found here. Before long a path can be seen below; gain this for some welcome easy walking, bearing left towards the **Pas de la Beccia**. A wonderful, old military shelter can be found before the pass on the main path. It has no door or facilities of any kind but is sheltered and easy to find. ◄ More boundary posts and barbed wire mark the top of the pass and the border in 1892. Looking up and back to the summit will certainly make you feel you are a hundred per cent mountaineer.

The shelter could be a good meeting point for a mixed ability party, one taking the ridge while the other takes a gentler walk from the fort along the track up the valley to the refuge.

There are two descent choices (or three if the route is reversed). The shortest and quickest route is to return along the military track, passing the shelter and continuing on down the valley to the fort and down to the car park. The path becomes a track and you could, if you prefer, follow this all the way down the valley until you meet a better track (almost unsurfaced road). Turn right and make your way to the road to the col, following it past the *fromagerie* at **la Ramasse** and up to the car park.

The alternative is to continue over the pass and follow the twisting descent path towards the **Lac du Mont Cenis**. The rough road is then taken to end up back at the col. A well-earned drink at the restaurant finishes off a fabulous day and lets you view the skyline route you have just completed.

ROUTE 20
Signal du Petit Mont Cenis

Time	8–9hrs
Distance	17km
Ascent	1300m
Map	3634OT Val Cenis
Start	GR 0335 5015
Parking	La Ramasse *fromagerie*
Grade	2 (Alpine PD-)

A route with a 'proper' Alpine grade (PD-), longer than you might think but never disappointing. The route is mainly on solid rock and very airy in places, and then you find firing platforms and a war memorial commemorating acts worthy of distinction!

Park near the *fromagerie* at la Ramasse, taking care not to park in the farm car park – a little further on there is an opportunity to park on the right on the verge. The track that passes the farm and gently climbs the hillside is an early warm-up for the day ahead. Cross the Pont Lapouge, an obvious bridge over the small stream, and continue for a short distance to a path signposted for La Turra. This path joins the old military track/road into Combe de Cléry; follow this towards the Pont Bonneval. Don't be tempted to take the streamside path, as it is a steeper climb to join the track later. ▸ Strike off across country to join the ever-improving obvious path that

Before the Pont Bonneval is an enormous boulder blocking the road, which obviously fell since the track was built!

Cime du Laro's north ridge in outline from the summit of Petit Signal du Mont Cenis

climbs to the Col des Randouillards. The path is exposed in places, and if this exposure is too much, now is the time to turn around, as the scramble only really begins after the col. A number of zigzags will gain the col, with Pointe de Cugne looming above.

From here, the ridge is obvious and the rough rock is welcome. These mountains are subjected to greater erosion forces than those in the UK and the routes are much less frequented. These facts combine to make the rock looser than on UK routes, so test crucial foot and hand holds before fully committing to them. The whole ridge to the top is a mixture of fabulous easy slabs and short steep descents that can be avoided if preferred, usually to the right of the ridge.

Having enjoyed the scramble to the summit of **Pointe de Cugne**, you are nicely warmed up for the ensuing adventure. Looking at times like a Torridon ridge and rising to 3162m, the section that follows is breathtaking in every sense. Pinnacles, exposure, slabs and airy steps abound and the rough nature of the rock is reassuring.

Faint markings can be found – the familiar red-and-white paint flashes urge you on, but the ridge is sufficient way-marking in itself. Keep to its top for the majority of the way, though you may find some downclimbs too challenging. If so, reverse your route a little and options to one side or the other (usually the right-hand side of the ridge) can be found.

When the summit of **Signal du Petit Mont Cenis** is reached it is worth trying to imagine how pitched battles were fought here; a memorial marks the fallen from both armies. The descent is via the easier west ridge to **Col de Sollières**. Follow the ridge from the summit, south first, then bearing right. A discernable path passes firing platforms built, presumably, for mountain infantry to use. A large white cross is visible near to the col. At the col there is a meeting of paths and tracks. Take the farm track signposted for l'Erellaz for an easy but long traverse to the ski lifts at le Sort de l'Erellaz. Descend a mixture of ski roads, paths and shortcuts to reach the restaurant/chair lifts at **Replat des Canons**. Locate the track signed 'Col du Mont Cenis 6km'. This pleasant tree-shaded track passes two memorials to troops killed by avalanches, before reaching Pont Lapouge and the track back to the farm.

High on the ridge above the clouds nearing the summit

ROUTE 21
Arête de Léché

Time	4½–5½hrs from refuge; 7–8hrs from dam
Distance	6km from refuge; 11km from dam
Ascent	920m from refuge; 1350m from dam
Map	3534OT Trois Vallées
Start	GR 0321 5016 (Refuge de la Dent Parrachée)
Parking	Car park at the dam wall, Plan d'Amont
Grade	PD-

This is a tough but wonderful route, with an incredibly photogenic shark's fin ridge and close-up views of the upper reaches of la Dent Parrachée. It shares the descent from the high col with the Route 22 and will therefore allow a degree of 'recceing' this route. With a high point of 3400m, starting from Plan d'Amont will mean a total ascent of over 1300m and a long day, but it is good preparation for an attempt on la Dent Parrachée. In the height of summer it is unlikely that much, if any, snow or ice will be encountered, although you should check local conditions with a refuge guardian. For very quick moving parties, or those prepared for an early start and late finish, it is possible to link this route with Route 22 to give a spectacular route on rock for mid-grade Alpinists that would rank as one of the best mountain days in the region.

As the route really starts at the Refuge de la Dent Parrachée, there are two options. The first is to stay at the refuge overnight and enjoy a leisurely start to the day. The refuge is very popular as it serves the GR5 and climbers attempting la Dent Parrachée so early booking is essential. Staying at the privately owned Refuge de la Fournache is an alternative. The second option is to start from the car park at the dam early in the morning and make the ascent to the refuge before beginning the route proper. The route is well trodden and clearly signposted.

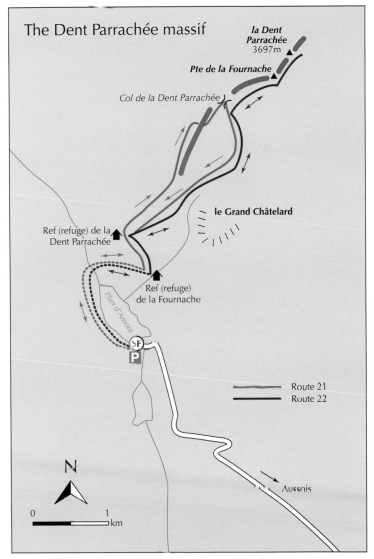

The Dent Parrachée massif

la Dent Parrachée 3697m

Pte de la Fournache

Col de la Dent Parrachée

le Grand Châtelard

Ref (refuge) de la Dent Parrachée

Ref (refuge) de la Fournache

Plan d'Amont

SF
P

Route 21
Route 22

N

0   1
km

Aussois

The shark's fin ridge of the Pointe de Leche route is a thrilling midpoint of the route

The summit of Pointe de Léché is a very impressive sight.

From the refuge locate the unsigned but well-trodden path straight up the hillside. It is worth locating the path the afternoon before if staying in the refuge. The path leads in a north-easterly direction and steadily gains height; before long the grass begins to give way to bare ground and a reasonably stable scree slope gains the ridge. The ridge gets better and better and passes a false summit to become much more exposed but thoroughly enjoyable. ◄

The view into the bowl between the two ridges ahead may be off-putting, but the route gains the right-hand ridge without as much height loss or difficulty as the view suggests. Continue along the ridge before crossing to the right across the boulder field to gain the right-hand ridge. This ridge is more challenging and is graded at PD-. It is exposed and steep and, in places, loose, as some parties only climb as far as Pointe de Léché. Pass to the left of a red tower (it looks like a lot of height may be lost to gain the tower, but this is not the case) and continue to the unnamed summit at 3400m. The view from here is magnificent and all the technical difficulties are now complete, the descent to the **Col de la Dent Parrachée** being straightforward.

The descent from the col demands care and respect, and a helmet is a wise precaution – it is loose in places and disturbed rocks can be lethal. Early in the season crampons may well be necessary, as the slope can hold snow until July or even later. A permanent snowfield exists on the lower section of the slope and makes a welcome change from the loose scree. Once the descent, is complete an intermittent path leads to the right past **le Grand Châtelard**, a huge bastion of rock. The myriad paths on the hillside all lead in the same general direction, but can be confusing to a tired group. The higher paths trending to the right lead towards the Refuge de la Dent Parrachée, while those heading more to the left trend towards the Refuge de la Fournache. After collecting any equipment left at the refuge (if you stayed there overnight) and enjoying a well-earned drink, the descent is a simple reverse of the ascent.

The short exposed summit ridge of Pointe de Léché

ROUTE 22
La Dent Parrachée

Time	Day 1: 2hrs; Day 2: 8–9hrs plus 1½hrs return to car park
Distance	12km
Ascent	1650m
Map	3534OT Trois Vallées
Start	GR 0321 5014
Parking	Car park at the dam wall, Plan d'Amont
Grade	PD

La Dent Parrachée dominates the upper valley. Its classic triangular shape and imposing stance towering over Termignon and Lanslebourg make it the Matterhorn of the valley. The vertical gain to the summit from Termignon is 2400m – higher than two Snowdons stacked on top of each other. It is barely 5km from Termignon to the summit of la Dent Parrachée and so the presence of this mountain is hard to ignore. To attain its summit is a significant achievement. The route involves steep scrambling, difficult scree slopes will challenge your perseverance and snow slopes protect the final ridge from all invaders. The altitude will begin to play a part in the final climb, but an early start and knowledge that there will be little snow to cross later in the day is comforting. Fit and experienced scramblers will thrill at climbing the mountain of the valley. Professional guides will willingly take less experienced mountaineers up the Voie Normale; this is the route described here and is a solid Alpine grade PD.

This is a true Alpine adventure and an Alpine start from the refuge is required. This will allow for a safe ascent to the Col de la Dent Parrachée, while everything is still frozen in place.

The first challenge of the day is to gain the path which passes le Grand Châtelard to its left. A number of paths lead from the refuges into the valley and it is worth identifying the route during the afternoon while relaxing

at the refuge of your choice. None of these paths are signposted, but all are well worn. After passing **le Grand Châtelard** the path becomes more and more distinct and arrives at the base of the steep scree slope leading to the col. This scree slope is a difficult climb, as it is loose and ever shifting; donning a helmet at this point is a wise precaution. The Rocher de Dame is a landmark on the slope. Pass to right of this significant pillar of rock – to the left is more difficult ground and the author was witness to an impressive helicopter rescue of a group unfortunate enough to have become separated and cragfast here. The route from the Dame is more easily seen zigzagging up the steepening slope and after substantial efforts the col is reached. Care must also be taken not to take the path further to the right which passes an orange-yellow rib; this route is even steeper and loose.

Close up view of Dent Parrachée and Pointe de la Fournache

103

From the col the route changes character. A path is apparent leading off to the right and crosses a short compacted scree slope. After this scree the climbing begins. The route is worn and crampon scratches are a steady waymarker. A few vertical bastions look intimidating, but these are invariably bypassed. A steep gully head is reached and a few zigzags on unconsolidated rock lead to a solid and reassuring ridge to the summit of **Pointe de la Fournache**. A slip above the gully could be very serious indeed and care must be taken along this section, but the climb to the ridge is on good holds which are incut and reassuring.

The view from the Pointe de la Fournache is fantastic and the short ridge to **la Dent Parrachée** (3697m) is the final challenge. A snow slope invariably exists between these two summits and crampons need to be donned to cross the slope safely: it falls away to the right and a slip must be avoided. With crampons fitted this becomes a simple crossing and a short rocky section finishes the climb to the summit. The summit view is stupendous: almost every other summit in this guidebook is visible and many Alpine greats are clearly visible. The view down to Termignon is dizzying; Mont Blanc is clearly visible; the Matterhorn and Monta Rosa can also be seen.

To descend, the route is reversed, which means recrossing the snow slope and descending the steep slopes to the col. Care must be taken, particularly in the traverse past the gully, but before too long the col is reached and the slopes down to le Grand Châtelard need to be tackled. These are long and tiring but it is soon possible to glissade down the gentle snow slopes and return to the refuge. As mentioned in Route 21, there are some minor problems of route finding to overcome before a celebratory drink can be enjoyed at the refuge.

The via ferrata is very much a recent phenomenon in France and has been developed with tourism as a major driving force. The routes are therefore well equipped, well signposted from car parks or roads and designed for thrills and excitement. The cabling and hardware are regularly maintained by the local councils and guides and are of a very high standard. To give you an indication of the difficulty there is a grading system, similar to Alpine grades in name/letters but not comparable in terms of difficulty. A via ferrata graded D is indeed difficile (difficult), but would not compare to the complex skills of route finding, gear placement and glacier crossing nor to the sheer length of route and time required to complete it of an Alpine D route. Grading is, in any case, subjective and depends on a number of factors. Your height will dictate how difficult some routes are and one of these routes (Route 28) has a minimum height requirement of 150cm. Some routes are designed with children in mind: they have rungs closer together with shorter reaches. The routes have a recognised 'one way system' and occasionally you will come across 'no entry' signs to ensure everyone follows the same routes – trying to pass people on via ferrata is very difficult and you get far too close to strangers in a multilingual game of Twister!

Equipment requirements are similar to rock climbing, with some vital differences. The most important of these is the self-belaying lanyard. There are a number of different styles on the market; most important of all is a good understanding of how to use the equipment safely. The special karabiners used are very important:

Stepping off a large flake high above the Arc river and Pont Diable (Route 27)

A correct via ferrata lanyard is a must. The auto-locking krabs open wider than normal ones.

they need to be wide opening and quick locking as you are constantly opening and closing them around wide cables. The equipment can be hired locally and is cheaper to buy in France than in the UK.

A climbing helmet and harness are essential. Other things you may consider are a rope to help your partner out on a difficult or exposed section; a couple of slings and a belay device could also be of value. You need to think about how to belay each other and have rehearsed such scenarios prior to undertaking a route at the upper end of your ability. A quick-draw clipped to the belay loop is really useful for clipping yourself to a rung for a rest on a steep section or for taking photographs. Children should be roped and belayed at all times as a mistake clipping the cable could be disastrous.

Other important things to consider are footwear and gloves. Gloves are very useful as the rungs and cables become uncomfortable – mountain biking gloves are very good as they have hardwearing palms and

106

ventilated backs. Footwear is another conundrum; many people wear trainers but if you have ever stood on ladders all day painting the house you'll be aware of how uncomfortable this becomes. Stiff but light boots are recommended and specific via ferrata shoes are also available.

Make sure everything is fastened down! Clip camera straps to harnesses or rucksacks – a dropped camera could be deadly to someone a few hundred metres below. Sunglasses should also be held on by some form of strap. Sunscreen, a drink and snacks are well worth carrying and a first aid kit should be taken.

If you are unsure about tackling a route or the skills involved in tackling via ferrata then going with a guide is to be recommended; climbers will quickly pick it up. Don't forget that falling is still dangerous even when clipped to a cable, as there are rungs, pig tails and cables to catch as well as the rock.

If you intend to self-lead via ferrata it is useful to read the excellent Petzl brochure (free from Petzl retailers or as a downloadable pdf of technical tips from the Petzl website www. petzl.com/en/outdoor) for information on how to belay, lead and protect via ferrata using their equipment. The diagrams are very good and much of the text is in English. Other chapters look at leading and seconding rock climbs and glacier travel. Further advice is printed on information boards at the start of most routes.

ROUTE 23
Le Pichet, Lanslevillard

Time	1–1½hrs
Map	3634OT Val Cenis
Start	GR 0337 5018
Parking	Lanslevillard: eastern side (up-valley road)
Grade	PD-

A great little route, graded PD and suitable for children over about 8 or 9 years. There is a bit of allsorts here: some rock to climb along, good protection, a stunning leaning ladder clearly visible from the road and a small suspension bridge, all within a short walk. Given its close proximity to the road you are unlikely to be alone; if solitude is sought an evening may be a better time to do this route.

From the artisan shop which sells sheepskins on the valley road out of Lanslevillard cross the road at the zebra crossing and follow the signs towards the base of the via ferrata cliff. This is apparent early on thanks to the ladder bolted onto the crag leaning out into space – an optional challenge on the route.

After gearing up you need to decide – ladder or no ladder? If you wish to avoid the ladder then continue along the path a short distance to find a cable and steep path joining the route after the roof and ladder section. To tackle the ladder and roof begin the route up the fairly steep and strenuous first section – a bit daunting, but as difficult as anything on the whole route. Traverse right to gain the base of the ladder and climb this, ensuring the cable is always clipped. A slightly awkward step off the ladder puts you on top of the roof. A traverse to the right allows good views into the valley and great photo opportunities. ▸

The option avoiding the ladder joins the route here.

Ascending the cable after completing the ladder

A steep section now follows and then a long, easy traverse on a narrow path. Don't be tempted to discard the cable, as a slip could be extremely serious. As the path turns rockier, a small ravine is encountered. The suspension bridge is the next challenge, a bit wobbly and good fun for the younger members of the party. A short ladder climbs a steep section, and a descending traverse followed by a steep descent to the path completes this fine little route. Follow the path back to the start of the route and return by the same footpath through the fields to Lanslevillard.

 ROUTE 24

The Pinnacles, Aussois

Time	40mins–1hr
Map	3534OT Trois Vallées
Start	GR 0324 5012
Parking	Le Croix, Aussois–Sardières road
Grade	AD

A very easy approach (as short as 20m from a car parking spot) and the spectacular nature of the route combined with the short time it takes to complete a circuit means this is a popular route. It is photogenic and challenging, but also offers plenty of escape opportunities and would serve as a bit of early evening entertainment or an arrival/departure day activity. Using via ferrata equipment to climb living trees is also an opportunity not to be missed!

Park at le Croix on the way out of Aussois and walk along the minor road towards the monoliths. It is possible to drive along here and park at the apex of the hairpin from which the route is signposted, but there is only parking for one or two cars and the walk is short enough (around 800m) to make this unnecessary. The sign at the hairpin indicates the route is 20m and unusually this is not time but distance! The pinnacles are seen immediately and the cable strung between them both apparent and inviting. Pass underneath the cable between the pinnacles and locate the beginning of the route: this is at the base of the right-hand pinnacle from the road. The route starts up

The traverse of the cables with one of the tree sections in the background

the cliff face, simple enough but steep, before crossing a short plank to gain the tree trunk.

The cable snakes around the trunk and the cut off branches form hand and footholds. Keeping the via ferrata slings over one arm to stop them from dragging and snagging below makes life considerably easier on this section. Another plank leads back to the cliff and a simple walk leads to the monkey bridge. Crossing this is simple yet exhilarating and leads to the descent of the other pillar. This may be done by either descending via another tree trunk or, more easily, by a route down the cliff.

ROUTE 25

Guy Favre, Balme Noir

Time	5hrs
Map	3633ET Haute Maurienne
Start	GR 0346 5023
Parking	Car park (signed VF) between Bonneval-sur-Arc and le Villaron
Grade	D

A long and more serious route, likely to take at least three hours, more like four, with another hour being needed for the descent. The weather needs to be settled and you should carry clothing to take into account the significant change in altitude. The 800m of ascent means this is more like a low-grade climbing adventure in the vertical world. The descent is also about 45mins of walking following a lovely stream and series of waterfalls. The altitude gain means you will end at around 2500m; if you are not acclimatised this route is likely to be more taxing than you might expect.

From the car park next to the via ferrata sign at the roadside locate a small path leading off to the left to the base of the cliffs. The path wends its way up steepening

ground. There is an option to complete a small, child-friendly route, the Parcours Pierre Blanc, or to take the path itself. Some cabling exists on the path and before long the route starts up the rock. After completing the first rock band, a path resumes trending to the left and climbing to the main rock face. The route is steep but the equipment is good and height is steadily gained.

The route gains a significant amount of height. The cars in the background give a sense of scale

Views down the valley steadily improve; make sure you take time to look around. The route continues upwards and takes some steep slabs head on; luckily there are plenty of rungs and steps to assist. As the route bears right, a plank spanning a short corner appears – pirates this high up? After crossing this the route climbs straight to the top of the cliff. A small, level grassy terrace is a delightful late lunch stop. ▸ The path leads into a wide gully and a beautiful waterfall is a pleasant diversion. The descent passes the climbing venue Drailles Blanches and crosses a couple of fields back to the car park.

Marmots can be seen up here if you sit quietly and patiently.

111

THE VICTOR EMMANUEL FORT COMPLEX

Map: 3534OT Trois Vallées
Start: GR 0322 5003

Probably the most impressive collection of via ferrata routes in France is the Via Ferrata du Diable at the Victor Emmanuel Fort complex. Routes can be combined to create anything from a 1hr route to a whole day of vertical adventure. Two routes (Les Angelots and Les Diablotins) traverse the fort's walls and are specifically designed for children, having shorter reaches and more closely spaced rungs.

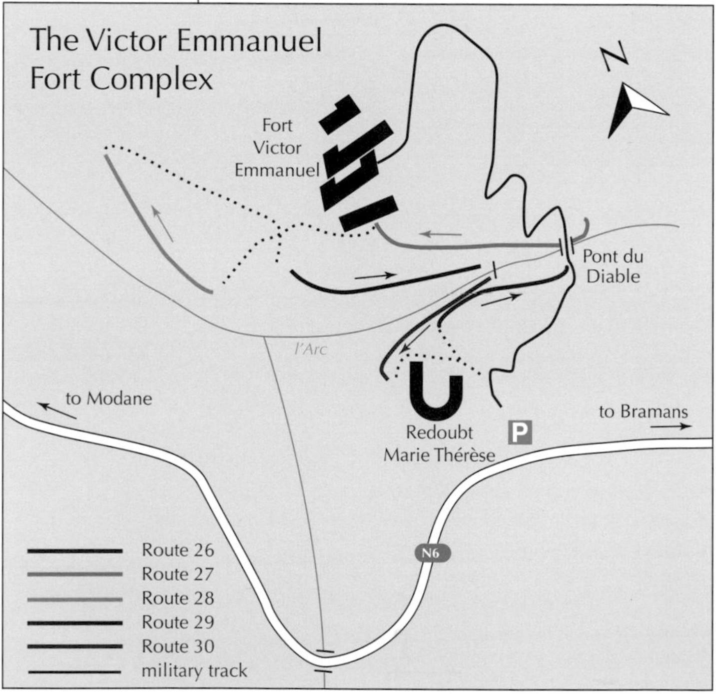

The Victor Emmanuel Fort Complex

Fort Victor Emmanuel

N

Pont du Diable

l'Arc

to Modane

to Bramans

Redoubt Marie Thérèse

P

N6

Route 26
Route 27
Route 28
Route 29
Route 30
military track

The routes are centred on the 200m deep gorge and the bridge spanning this gap, in places only about 30m wide. Most of the routes are on the Victor Emmanuel Fort side, while the Redoute Marie Thérèse is the site of a reasonably sized car park, toilets, café and adventure park. Parking is free, as is access to the routes.

From the car park the old military road descends to the Pont du Diable, the Devil's Bridge, which then climbs to the Victor Emmanuel Fort across the gorge.

ROUTE 26
Traversée des Anges

Time	1–1½hrs
Grade	D

The Angel's Traverse is a strange route as it is predominately a descent. It has a few steep climbs en route to the Pont du Diable; if the route is proving too challenging there is an escape option part way through.

This route starts from a platform/gateway close to the car park at the Redoute Marie Thérèse. From the car park, walk downhill behind the fort through the adventure course, bearing slightly left to a gateway and information board. There is a viewing point here and usually a number of sightseers so you are unlikely to be alone!

Clip onto the cable and walk around the corner to begin the first descent. This descent becomes a descending traverse and encounters a strenuous, slightly overhanging section of traverse. There is the option of escaping after this point, as the next part is more strenuous. Continue traversing and descending before a climb with some overhanging sections, then a final vertical section brings you to the end of the traverse. A short path joins

The route is well equipped with rungs and cabling

the bridge track; this wide track leads uphill from the bridge back to the car park. If you want more then cross the bridge for the next route (Route 27) which is similar in difficulty but with more climbing involved.

 ROUTE 27
Montée au Ciel

Time	1–1½hrs
Grade:	D

The Montée au Ciel, or Climb to the Sky, is a great route, with increasing exposure and sustained climbing making this route a great challenge. The unique finish, which uses a gun port of the fort, adds a final twist to the journey.

Cross the Pont du Diable and locate the cable/gateway just to the right of the bridge. Follow the cable under the bridge and begin the upward climb. A few vertical or slightly overhanging sections lead towards an enormous block. Step from this back onto the cliff and a final vertical/overhanging section leads to the most interesting way into the Victor Emmanuel Fort – via a gun port.

Before entering the gun port, two choices present themselves. Turn left and follow the cables outside the fort to join the other routes described below or enter the fort and walk back to the bridge and on to the car park.

If you plan to do the classic circuit then the path to the left beckons. This is also the path to Les Rois Mages (The Three Kings), the toughest route in this section.

The route back to the car park is via the gun port. Enter the port, which narrows as you climb into the fort. Make your way uphill along a series of tunnels and walkways to the main entrance. Cross the moat (look down to see the children's routes traversing the fort's walls) and take care not to miss the path on the right towards Pont du Diable.

The Victor Emmanuel Fort complex

❻ ROUTE 28
Les Rois Mages

Time	45mins–1hr
Grade:	TD

What a route! Three challenging bridges named after The Three Kings make a substantial and strenuous route. The rock sections between the bridges are vertical or overhanging, adding to the difficulty of the route. The bridges span great drops with considerable exposure, making for a short but thrilling route. An escape path after the first and easiest bridge allows those who find they have bitten off more than they can chew to make a dignified exit.

The longest suspension bridge on a route in France at 83m long

The path from the fort towards the Descente aux Enfers enters some woodland after a small stream line. There is a via ferrata signpost on the path in the woods that explains the route. Clip onto the cable and descend awkwardly

onto the 25m Himalayan bridge. A strenuous overhanging section leads around the corner and continues for around 20m. There are few let-ups on this section and a quick-draw could be a useful rest aid. As the second bridge is reached the option to escape offers itself.

Bear in mind that the majority of the overhanging sections are now completed; one short overhanging section joins the last two bridges. But now the monkey bridge awaits. The cables are taut and are set to make you traverse the bridge facing outwards towards the abyss! The rock is still steep to overhanging leading to the final bridge, which is an 83m suspension bridge – the longest on a route in France. Paint dots mark the way back to the path. Either continue down to the next route (Route 29) or climb back up to the fort.

ROUTE 29

Descente aux Enfers

Time	40mins–1hr
Grade	D

The 'Descent to Hell' is a short route which is probably best described as a link route but nevertheless has some exciting moments and ends at a suspension bridge in the depths of the gorge, a rather claustrophobic position after the exposed walls of the earlier routes.

From the fort follow the path to the left. It follows the wall round the corner and then descends along a rough path to a wood. The path picks its way through the woods and then steepens to a cabled via ferrata. The route begins as a descending traverse, changing into a more vertical descent. The main difficulties are some slight overhangs before a suspension bridge over the river is reached. The

The river upstream of the crossing

gorge is narrow here and Indiana Jones films will no doubt spring to mind. Cross the bridge to begin the next route, no other exit options exist.

ⓑ ROUTE 30

Remontée au Purgatoire

Time	1 hour
Grade:	D

The Return to Purgatory is a straightforward but steep and strenuous rising traverse which climbs out of the depths of the gorge. It begins where the previous route left off, the suspension bridge crossing the Arc river.

The route begins with a rising traverse, and after rounding a corner of trees things steepen up. More rising traversing brings you close to the waterfall. The route follows the left-hand side of the waterfall and steepens to vertical. Depending upon the weather on the previous few

It is reassuring to know the routes are well maintained!

days the waterfall may be a roaring cascade or a subdued trickle. Some overhanging sections lead to the end of the route under a suspension bridge. Be very careful near the top: do not be tempted to paddle in the stream bed – it is slippery and a slip could result in a fatal fall over the waterfall. The path through the trees returns to the car park in about 5mins.

ROUTE 31

Via Cordatta, Col de la Madeleine

Time	2–2½hrs
Map	3633ET Haute Maurienne
Start	Col de Madeleine
Grade	III (mixed VF and climbing, see below)

This is not a via ferrata route but blends via ferrata styles with climbing. The route has no cabling whatsoever, but uses 'pigtails' (which allow the lead climber to create running belays quickly) and iron work for protection. A rope is an absolute essential, along with some basic climbing skill, as is the ability to use belay chains and to be comfortable with hanging belays.

This is a great route for speeding up and fine-tuning rope work for long rock routes where leading through is an essential skill for both climbers. It can also serve as a challenging route in its own right and at 16 pitches in length it will prove a good afternoon's sport. Graded III, in climbing terms this means the hardest sections are around Diff–V Diff by UK standards. The signpost recommends a rope of at least 30m, but this will necessitate moving together roped up, so 50m is more practical. Belay devices, slings and some karabiners will also be required, and a couple of quickdraws may prove useful for quick attachment to the rungs encountered en-route.

Parking at the Blocs de Madeleine car park will allow for a shorter walk back after finishing the route and an opportunity to inspect the crag whilst walking to the start.

Pigtails are the in situ protection for this route

The other option is to park at the junction of the minor road and main valley road near the top of the switchbacks from Lanslevillard. Do not be tempted to park on this minor road as the gendarmes patrol the area and enforce the no parking rule.

From le Collet walk down the road, passing under the long cliff. The route makes a rising traverse of this cliff and other groups may be visible. Do not be tempted to cross the fields too early to gain the base of the cliff, a rough scrabble through thorny bushes awaits. A path and signs lead to the start of the route.

The first pitches are easy enough and will familiarise the leader in using pigtails effectively. Hooking through them one way is very easy, whereas trying to attach to them incorrectly will become apparent as it is difficult and the rope will drop out. Be sure to practise this before moving further along the route. A few pitches lead to a grassy corner and a short walk along a narrow path, passing the course of a waterfall. This walk will necessitate moving together roped up, or a longer rope than the signpost recommended 30m.

A magnificent position for a hanging belay

The second section of the route brings more exhilarating climbing, with some vertical sections and numerous exposed positions. It may well be tempting to run some pitches together but rope drag will become a factor and make progress more tiring. Some hanging belays offer spectacular photo opportunities and the pitches lead to a short downclimbing section. Thereafter follows a final rising traverse before the ground gives way to greenery and a path. From the top of the route the path leads both left and right. Turning right leads back to le Collet in about 15mins.

4 ROCK CLIMBING

Rock climbing in France is very different to the UK climbing scene; these mainly sports climbs are usually bolted or planned for easy top roping. This means less equipment is needed than in the UK. Routes often have names painted on the bottom of each route, making it much easier to decipher guidebook pictures and topos. Solid rock and a sunny climate are also valuable assets!

To climb on these routes you will need the following:

- single rope – 60m is the best, some routes are longer than 25m so a lower-off needs 60m unless you are competent at climbing on double ropes and setting a lower-off with them.
- harness
- shoes
- chalk bag
- quickdraws (about 12)
- belay device
- screwgate karabiners
- short sling to attach yourself to the lower-off point while setting up the lower.

The short sling is usually attached to the harness belay loop with a lark's foot and has a screwgate krab on the other end. On reaching the top of the route, clip into the chain or ring bolt with this sling before untying and rethreading the rope for a lower-off. Some people use a couple of leftover quickdraws for this task. Many routes, but not all, now have a strong sprung maillon at the top of the routes, meaning this procedure is unnecessary.

Note All climbs in this book are lower-offs, usually on snaplinks, so there is no need to rethread for most (but not absolutely all). It is good practice to take a loop of rope and tie it off to your harness before untying the rope for the lower-off, then should you fumble the rope during the untie-rethread-retie routine it doesn't disappear down the crag and leave you high on a crag with no possible method of descent.

Helmets are a personal choice: very few will be found wearing them on these crags other than children under instructor guidance. Only you can decide on this issue, but bear in mind young children and inexperienced climbers may drop kit from above.

Gradings are French sports grades, commonly in use on UK climbing walls, and take no account of exposure as they are well bolted. As a rough guide, take two technical grades off the UK grade to give a French equivalent, so a French 3c equates to around Diff–V Diff, French 4c is about UK 4a (Hard Severe) and 5c in French is about 5a (HVS to E1) in the UK.

These venues vary in nature but all share a relaxed, family feel. Three

Solid rock and sunshine make for a pleasant afternoon's climbing at Rocher des Amoureux

of them are popular with groups, but they are also the two closest to roads so make a great evening venue when the climbing schools have gone home.

The valley is smothered with crags, many sharing low to mid-grade routes, others having routes up to F8a. Higher up the mountains you can find long multi-pitch routes needing more

124

traditional climbing skills and equipment. The definitive guidebook, *Topo Escalade en Maurienne* by Patrick Col, is available in book shops in the valley. It is written in French but has topos and photo guides for each venue and covers 46 different venues, plus mountain routes and bouldering sites.

🐾 ROUTE 32
Rocher des Amoureux

Map	3534OT Trois Vallées
Location:	GR 0319 5009

A popular crag close to Modane and served by a nearby car park and toilets makes this a busy, sociable place to climb. Groups of children under instruction as young as five years old will be found on the easy routes, while family groups and older climbers cruising the mid grades will abound. There are over 100 routes here varying from 3c to 8a, though the vast majority are between 4b and 5c. Leaving kit unattended is probably not a wise move but the close proximity to the car park means spare kit can easily be locked away.

The easier sections tend to be in the shade in the morning and get the full sun in the afternoon. As the routes are equipped by the local instructors, it is expected that they have priority on access with groups.

Families enjoy an afternoon on the rock

Rocher des Amoureux

1 Relax Max 4a
2 Bigbag 5a
3 Gomme d'Adam 4c

4 Fastoch 4c
5 Rock à manouilles 4a
6 Mamma mia 4a

7 Tornicoti tornicoton 4a
8 Capricorne 3c

Directions From Modane take the road (D215) to Aussois, which passes under the railway and crosses the Arc via a bridge. The road climbs past the entrance of the Fort Saint-Gobain to a roundabout. The crag is obvious as you approach the roundabout and parking is off this roundabout.

ROUTE 33
Sollières

Map	3634OT Val Cenis
Location	GR 0328 5014

You could literally belay from the car at this popular site. Groups are often found using the crag and it can therefore get quite busy. The evenings are, in contrast, usually deserted and as it has no walk in this makes it perfect for a few early evening routes. The solid and reliable rock provides good friction and is geologically interesting: a coarse conglomerate means each hand and foothold is very different. ▶

The routes at this venue vary from a really short 3c route to routes in the 6b–c category. Some routes are 10m, others are as long as 35m two-pitch routes. The quietest routes are to the left; follow the small dirt path steeply uphill for about 15m to discover a sort of cave, with routes to the right-hand side above the obvious lower cave.

Directions Follow the signposts from the main valley road (N6) to the Sollières airport (Aérodrome de Sollières-Sardières). The crag faces the tiny grass airstrip.

From within the furthest depths of the upper cave there are also some good routes (if a little awkward to start), graded at 4c–5a.

Conglomerate is essentially nature's concrete. A mixture of rocks and boulders held together in a matrix, each rock and boulder will be a different rock from elsewhere.

Sollières

1 Bilbo 5a	5 Tourneube 4a 5c	9 2001 5c
2 Arc en ciel 5c+	6 Solo en rut majeur 5c+	10 Fole de Roi 5b
3 Aeroplane blinde 5c+	7 Roro 5c+	11 Flo's garden 4c
4 Bouib's 4b	8 Hobbit 4b	

ROUTE 34
Rocher de Termignon

Map	3634OT Val Cenis
Location	GR 0329 5016

Although only a small crag on the edge of Termignon, this is worthy of an evening's climbing and only a short walk from the centre of the village. The routes seem hard for their grade (French 4b and upwards) and the crag is steep. It has been equipped and is maintained by the local guides, who

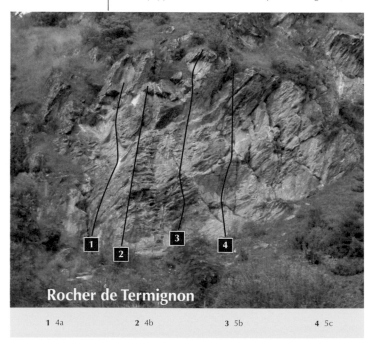

Rocher de Termignon

1 4a	**2** 4b	**3** 5b	**4** 5c

have the right of use over it with groups. They need at least four routes left free, which is effectively most of the crag, although the author has yet to see any group climbing there.

Directions From the centre, walk out of the village towards Lanslebourg for about 15m, taking the small road on the right with the ski hire shop on its corner. Take Rue de la Favière, following it as it switchbacks uphill. Pass a very nice house with a large garden – the crag is behind the garden. Carry on along the road for 20–30m, then take a small path on the right of a green shed.

A cable along the top of the crag allows you to set top ropes for routes once you've got up one route. You'll need 9–10 extenders and a 50m rope will be fine.

There is no parking on the approach road so please ensure you use the parking in the village.

ROUTE 35

Blocs de la Madeleine

Map	3633ET Haute Maurienne
Location	GR 0339 5018

This is another great venue with a short approach and pleasant shaded aspect. The blocs are perfect for lower grade climbers and novices, excellent quality schist gives great friction and the routes are all short. This means it is popular with instructor-led groups but perfect for an evening's entertainment. Routes are around 10m–15m in height and are equipped for leading on the main block, apart from routes 1 and 2 which are top rope routes less than 10m in height. The others are set up for leading but easy access to the top means you can top rope these routes too.

Directions Follow the main road up the valley towards Bessans from Lanslevillard. Some steep hairpins lead out of Lanslevillard to gain the Col de la Madeleine.

Blocs de la Madeleine (Routes 1–7)

1 4b	3 4b	5 4b	7 5b
2 4b	4 4b	6 4c	

Ignore a small road leading to le Collet and carry on for around 600m; a reasonably large lay-by on the left is the parking place (signed 'Rocher d'Escalade de la Madeleine'). The signed path leads from here into the woods; follow this to arrive at the blocs after a short distance (around 5mins walk).

None of the routes are named on the blocks.

Blocs de la Madeleine (Routes 8–10)

8 5c   9 6a   10 5a

ROUTE 36
Dalles du Mollard

Map	3633ET Haute Maurienne
Location	GR 0339 5019

Dalles du Mollard

1 Greenland 4b 5b   3 4b
2 4b   4 Barbarodrome 4b 6c

These slabs are clearly visible from the road and because there is a walk in to the crag you are virtually guaranteed to have the place to yourself. It sits on the GR5 so there are plenty of passers-by to admire your efforts! The rock is a fabulous schist slab which offers great friction and is tilted to a steep but not too difficult angle. It is in the full sun for much of the day so dries very quickly, but in the wet the rock loses its friction very quickly indeed and a rapid retreat is advised. As it is close to the Blocs de Madeleine it is a good alternative if a group is in situ there.

Directions Park at the lay-by/rough car park area as for the Blocs de Madeleine and pick a path through the shrubbery to the little hamlet of le Collet (or Hameau de la Madeleine as the sign in the hamlet calls it). The GR5 threads an easy-to-see path from the village up to the crag.

The two leading routes (both two pitches long) are Greenland and Barbarodrome. You could lead the first pitch then lower off or set a top rope for the other routes. A 60m rope is advised for the lower-offs – 50m is too short!

ROUTE 37
Drailles Blanches

Map	3633ET Haute Maurienne
Location	GR 0346 5023

This fine crag is set in a beautiful meadow and enjoys shade in the afternoon. The routes have a very relaxed, family atmosphere and your efforts will be admired by returning via ferrata climbers. The gneiss rock is polished in places, the belaying is comfortable and some large belay boulders have rings to help those weighing less than their partners. Routes are equipped with lower-off

1 Galerie d'Asterix 4b	4 Rintintin	7 Minetto 5a
2 Casimodo 4b	5 Hari Kiri 4c	8 Rock in chair 5a
3 Captain Haddock 4b	6 Marlinou 4c	9 Moussaillon 5b

points and are up to 25m in height. This crag shares the same car park as the Guy Favre via ferrata route and is a few minutes' walk from the car park.

To the left routes get generally progressively harder, Frisson at 6c+ being the hardest. Other notable routes on the left are Obelix (5c) and Indiana Jones (6a).

5 MOUNTAIN BIKING

The Upper Maurienne has a great range of tracks and trails to entice the cross-country mountain biker. Long climbs, technical descents and sweeping panoramas reward the keen and fit mountain biker. Clearly marked gently undulating trails can be found in the valley bottom, allowing less regular cyclists and families to enjoy an off-road adventure. There are no bridleways in France and off-road cycling is tolerated much more readily. The National Park, however, specifically forbids riding in the park anywhere other than the access route into the Femma Refuge.

There is the option for those keen on tough, steep, downhill routes to buy a day pass at different ski lift stations to allow unlimited mechanical uplifts and adrenaline-fuelled descents all day but to really explore the valley a full suspension XC-biased machine will probably be the tool for the job.

BIKE HIRE AND BIKE SHOPS

There are a number of sports shops all along the valley that rent mid-range hardtail MTBs from half a day through to a whole week. The fees are reasonable and the majority of bikes are LaPierre, a brand gaining respect in the MTB press and based at nearby Lyon. Some shops also stock premium models at a higher rental rate. A credit card will be required to act as a deposit for rentals – the shops will generally take a swipe of the card and charge for the bike should the bike be lost or damaged beyond repair (and don't generally sell insurance). Many shops also stock a reasonable range of spares but there are no 'full-on' bike shops, so it may be worth taking spare disc pads if your bike has exotic or specialist components. One of the best shops for parts and a range of hire bike sizes is the Inter Sport shop on the high street of Lanslevillard le Haut.

Singletrack leading into the descent to le Coin

THE ROUTES

There are a number of waymarked trails in the area. These are colour coded in a similar format to ski runs and a very useful map is available from tourist information centres throughout the valley. It is worth taking a 1:25,000 or 1:50,000 map as well.

Green routes: generally simple tracks with fairly good surfaces, usually farm tracks or forest fire trails.

Ascent is not too arduous (but may feel tough enough before acclimatisation). Distance will be around 8–15km and ascent around 100–200m. These routes are likely to be less than half a day in length. A hybrid bike or non-suspension MTB will cope with these routes.

Blue routes: these routes have more climbing and are longer. The routes will most likely mix fire trails for climbing and some more technical

Ski lifts help to make riding less strenuous and allow those with limited mobility a chance to join in

descents. Descents are steeper than green routes, but the surfaces are still likely to be reasonably compact and uniform. Distances and ascent will be greater, with routes being around 15km in length and ascent gains of around 250–400m. Regular cyclists will complete these routes within half a day or feel comfortable combining two into a day ride. Front suspension is recommended.

🚵 Red routes: steep and long climbs will be rewarded with technical or equally steep descents. Climbs will take upwards of an hour and the total ascent will be several hundred metres. At around 25–40km they may not be particularly long, but little of this will be on the level. Climbs tend to be on hard-packed fire trails, while descents may pick a line through the woods on single-track paths or be longer length descents on rough fire trails. A full suspension bike and disc brakes will make the ride a lot more enjoyable, as will an acclimatised cardio-vascular system and suitable experience to ride for 4–5hrs.

🚵 Black routes: tough! Usually over 1000m of climbing and very technical descents that require considerable experience. Certain descent sections will be very difficult and may well require 'porterage' for all but the most capable rider. All-mountain bikes will be well suited to these rides offering greater travel for the inevitable drop-offs. The routes will be over 40km in length and will take most of the day – pack a lunch and start early to make sure the big climbs are completed before it gets too warm.

The weather in the mountains can have a huge impact on cyclists, probably more so than for walkers. Long descents will cause significant wind chill and when combined with rain can bring on hypothermia remarkably quickly. Pack a windproof jacket! On a hot day be sure to pack enough water, as few of these routes have opportunities to replenish drinks bottles. Take some high-energy snacks, as well as a first aid kit to cope with any injuries, bumps and scratches. Spare inner tubes, a pump and a small toolkit are bike essentials (and not always provided by the hire shop!). A proper map and GPS/compass may prove invaluable, along with a mobile phone. Remember that it is easy to get sunburned cycling, as the air flow will make the ambient temperature cooler and so the effect of the sun's heat may go unnoticed.

A final point to bear in mind is that some sections of road riding are inevitable: be sure to observe the French rules of the road. It must be said that the French drivers are much more respectful of cyclists and will honk their horn from a distance away to warn of their imminent arrival – this is a friendly act rather than the more usual 'get out the way' attitude of many British motorists. They tend to allow plenty of room when overtaking too; cycling is far more pleasurable in France!

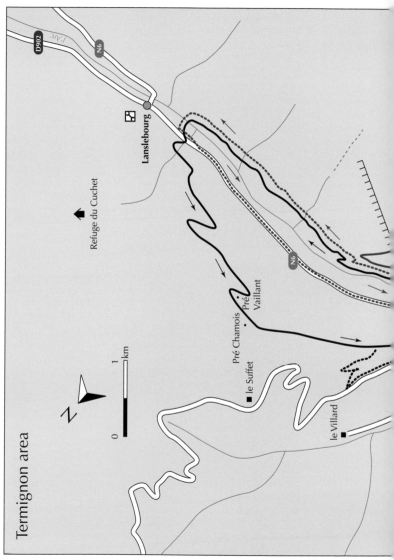

Termignon area

Refuge du Cuchet

Lanslebourg

D902

N6

L'Arc

N6

Pré Vaillant

Pré Chamois

le Suffet

le Villard

N

0   1 km

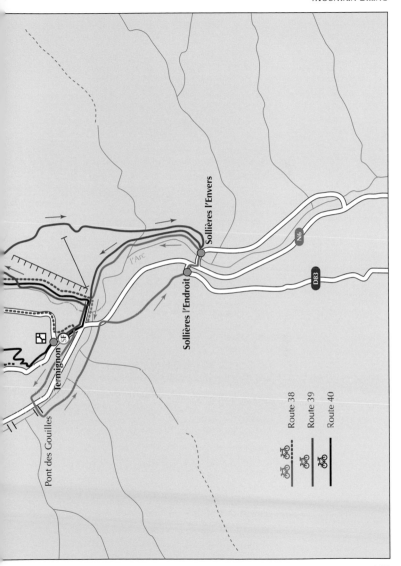

Sollières l'Envers

Sollières l'Endroit

l'Arc

N6

D83

Termignon

Pont des Gouilles

Route 38
Route 39
Route 40

ROUTE 38
Termignon and Sollières Circuit

Time	1–1½hrs or 1½ to 2hrs depending on options taken
Distance	7.5–18km
Ascent	120m or 330m
Map	3634OT Val Cenis
Start	Termignon village centre
Grade	Green (7.5km, 120m ascent); Blue (18km, 330m ascent)

This route avoids long climbs and technical trails. It is suitable for those with limited cycling skills and those who are occasional cyclists. It is mostly on good tracks and minor roads, bumpy in places, with an option to cut it short at halfway round before the 200m climb.

From Termignon locate the road bridge over the Doron on the west side of the village on the N6 (the main road down the valley). Take the minor road on the eastern side of the river (signed to the campsite) and follow this to the **Pont des Gouilles**. Cross the bridge and take the rough track back towards Termignon, with inspiring views on the right. The route both to and from the bridge is signposted with Green 10 cycle signage. The track becomes metalled again as it nears Termignon. It rejoins the main valley road at the Doron bridge. This very short loop would, on its own, be a great challenge to young children.

The route takes a rising dirt track, which forks right from the main road after about 70m. A gentle climb is rewarded with an exhilarating but straightforward descent into **Sollières l'Endroit** on a stony track. This is again signposted Green 10. The track becomes a rough road as it enters Sollières, turn left and downhill at the

The Chemin du Petit Bonheur wending its way through pastures

road (the Green 10 signposting is indistinct here but the route is straight through the hamlet). After a short distance the main (and sometimes busy) road is reached. Turn right and then take a left turn over the bridge towards **Sollières l'Envers** (signage is still Green 10, but the most apparent is for the campsite). Many cycle routes follow the next section, which is also a popular footpath, the Chemin du Petit Bonheur. The track is well signed on the left and climbs past the fishing ponds and little lakes. A pleasant track crosses pasture land towards the ski lifts at Termignon, and it is possible to end the route here if time is pressing. ▶

This little route would be a great starter route for young children or as a short ride.

To continue this route now involves a more difficult second part, which takes the Chemin du Petit Bonheur to Lanslebourg. Traverse above the apartment blocks to gain the rising metalled road, signed Blue 23. When the road splits, take the left fork onto a rougher track that levels out across meadows. A long climb follows on a forest trail, at times steep enough to notice the altitude at 1500m. After a couple of kilometres the path meets another at an obvious traffic sign, the highest point of the route. Follow the

Black 24 signs (this is not a difficult track but is sustained downhill at a gentle gradient). Take care – this is a popular walking trail and it is easy to pick up a lot of speed. As the track approaches **Lanslebourg** a few sharp hairpins offer a final flourish before tarmac takes over. From the middle of the town, the road back to **Termignon** is something of an enigma. It seems downhill almost all the way back, yet if travelled in the opposite direction the same is true (after the stiff climb out of Termignon).

 ROUTE 39

La Girarde

Time	2–2½hrs
Distance	8km
Ascent	460m
Map	3634OT Val Cenis
Start	Termignon village centre
Grade	Blue

A long climb is rewarded with an equally long descent that rarely involves technical skills. On a Tuesday, all the climbing can be avoided by using the chairlift!

From Termignon take the road to the ski lifts and keep on the metalled road, passing the apartment blocks. This is the Chemin du Petit Bonheur, Blue 23. The road climbs and at a junction take the left fork, again Blue 23. This level road crosses the summer meadows before turning into a rough track and starting a climb of a couple of kilometres to a road sign in the forest prohibiting motorised traffic beyond that point. Once this junction is reached, follow the Red 8 and Blue 23 signs upwards. Before too long the ski lift station la Girarde is reached and the

The wooden footbridge spanning the gorge

climbing is over. Continue following Blue 23 signs down-hill around some hairpins and more open corners.

At the point where the Blue 23 leaves the main track carry straight on. This track is rougher in places but never too technical and soon a magnificently crafted wooden bridge crosses a steep ravine, inviting a break to admire the gully both up and down stream. The track continues its downhill run all the way to **Sollières l'Envers**, looping around the back of the campsite to join the Chemin du Petit Bonheur. Follow this well-signed path easily back to Termignon, as described in Route 38.

🚲 ROUTE 40
Champions' Loop

Time	3hrs
Distance	17km
Ascent	660m
Map	3634OT Val Cenis
Start	Termignon village centre
Grade	Black

This might not seem far – 17km is a little over 10 miles – but much of it is a never-ending climb in the sun, followed by a tough and technical descent to test the most capable bike handlers. One for the champions!

From Termignon take the road to the ski lifts and keep on the metalled road past the apartment blocks to pick up the Chemin du Petit Bonheur, or take the N6 road to reach the village of **Lanslebourg**. Here the route begins in earnest by taking the road which passes the Baroque Museum church and Espace Multimedia library (or climbing the ramped path to the library more directly). Passing to the right of the Espace Multimedia the road climbs steadily and bears left. This rough road is signed 'Combe Sainte Marie' – follow this to locate Black 24 signs. A very old stone cross marks the way and the road turns into a dirt track. The track climbs steadily for an hour or so to eventually gain the **Pré Vaillant**. A little further sees the **Pré Chamois** reached and signage (Black 24) indicating the route descends to the left. Now the technical skills take over as steep ground, rocks and roots form the early part of the descent. This soon changes to less technical single-track, but with a steep grass slope on the left creating a considerable feeling of exposure.

Open grassland and rooty forest tracks lead down to a transmitter pylon at le Coin. There is the option to bail

out onto the vehicle access track at this point and join the minor road descending to Termignon. The other option is to continue on the Black 24 for more steep downhill with some very tight corners before hitting a forest trail. Follow this left (downhill) to join the minor road to **Termignon**. A champion's ride indeed!

Single track leading into the descent to le Coin

ROUTE 41
Chemin du Petit Bonheur

Time	5–6hrs round trip
Distance	58km
Ascent	800m
Map	3633ET Haute Maurienne
Start	Termignon village centre
Grade	Red

A great chance to see much of the upper valley, this route passes a number of villages, small chapels and archaeological sites. Some long and tough climbs make it a ride suitable for regular cyclists. As it follows the valley there are a number of opportunities to gain the road and cut the route short should the weather turn inclement.

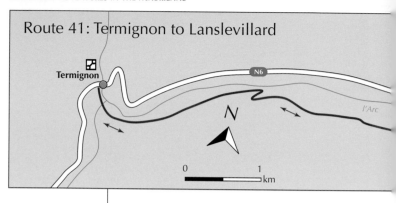

Route 41: Termignon to Lanslevillard

Termignon

N6

l'Arc

N

0   1
km

Les Marrons were the guides who directed sledges down the Col du Mont Cenis before the Fell railway was developed over the pass.

From Termignon take the road to the ski lifts and keep on the metalled road passing the apartment blocks. This is the Chemin du Petit Bonheur, Blue 23. The road climbs and at a junction take the left fork, signed Blue 23. This level road crosses the summer meadows before turning into a rough track and starting a climb of a couple of kilometres to a road sign in the forest prohibiting motorised traffic beyond that point. The long descent (Black 24) arrives at **Lanslebourg** after a few exhilarating zigzags. This will be 30–40mins of riding and a nice warm up. (Taking the valley road from Termignon to Lanslebourg will save about 20mins.) As the forest tracks open out keep on the south side of the river (its left bank) and follow the new road under ski lifts, following Green 25 and passing les Petit Marrons children's club. ◄ This minor road joins the main one before a roundabout and the *télécabine* (cable car) station at **Lanslevillard**. Leave the main road to climb to Lanslevillard l'Envers. The road passes apartment blocks before reaching a road junction by the church.

The outdoor and cycle shop on the left is the best stocked in the area.

Take the road on the right uphill along the main shopping street. ◄ Follow the Chemin du Petit Bonheur signage (also signed Green 16). The road continues to climb and turns into a dirt track, passing Chapelle St Etienne. A break here to admire the view will be welcome, as there is much more uphill to come. Green 16 signs are followed

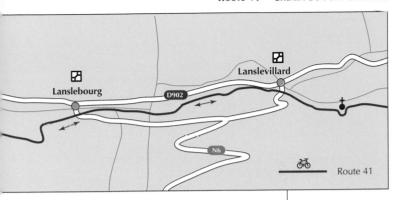

past some chalets and a small climbing venue. Beware that the signage for Green 16 takes the right choice at

The bridge at La Goulaz with the Pointe de Charbonnel as a backdrop

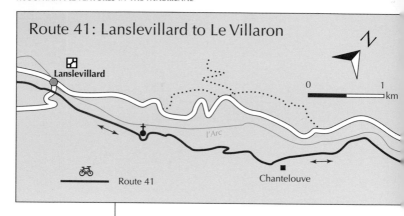

Route 41: Lanslevillard to Le Villaron

Lanslevillard

l'Arc

0   1
       km

Chantelouve

Route 41

a path junction, but you should stick to the Chemin du Petit Bonheur, which takes the left. The Chemin continues to climb remorselessly, eventually gaining the high point above the chalets of Chantelouve en Haut at 1770m. A long and welcome descent now follows. As the track leaves the forest, the route takes a sharp turn right onto Blue 17 (easy to miss). Overshooting this point will result

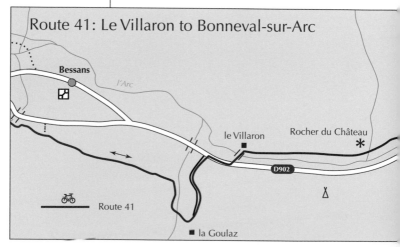

Route 41: Le Villaron to Bonneval-sur-Arc

Bessans

l'Arc

le Villaron   Rocher du Château
                              *

D902

Route 41

■ la Goulaz

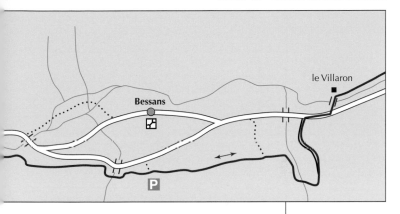

in joining the road by a bridge over the Arc river. The Blue 17 trail follows the road through forest before veering off into the Ribon valley to cross the river over a side-less bridge. A small picnic spot on the left in a clearing as the track veers away may be a pleasant lunch spot.

After crossing the bridge, turn left and follow the track uphill signed Blue 17, cross another bridge and

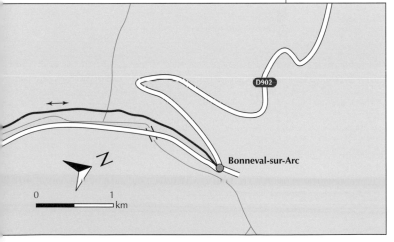

turn left to the main road. On joining the road, turn right up the valley for a short distance before taking the road on the left over a rickety-looking wooden bridge to **le Villaron**. The bridge is perfectly strong enough for bikes but cars are not allowed to use it.

The Chemin du Petit Bonheur is signed on the right to **Rocher du Château**. This is a popular track leading to rock paintings believed to be Neolithic. After having tried to decipher the faint images on the rock, continue along the path, which becomes single-track and technical for a short distance and may well involve a bit of pushing for 100m or so. The path is delightful from here to **Bonneval-sur-Arc** twisting through meadows and echoing to the shrill call of the marmot. All too soon Bonneval-sur-Arc is reached and a well-deserved coffee awaits. The village is a protected area and is deemed one of the most beautiful in France. Arriving at midday will mean it is inevitably busy but an hour or so exploring the backstreets and ancient roads is worthwhile.

To return there are numerous options. The easiest is by the road, which will take about 1–1½hrs, making for a total ride of 5hrs. Reversing the route will take around 2½hrs, meaning the ride will take 6hrs or so. The other option is to blend some road and some of the off-road sections enjoyed on the outward journey.

ROUTE 42
The Sardières Monolith

Time	4–5hrs
Distance	26km
Ascent	580m
Map	3634OT Val Cenis and 3534OT Trois Vallées
Start	Termignon village centre
Grade	Red

Long climbs and even longer descents will test you on this route. Some technical single track leads to a fabulous vantage point of the remarkable Monolithe de Sardières. Suitable for regular cyclists or those prepared for a challenge. The VTT-FFC map indicates that this ride begins at Aussois but this results in a long climb to finish; doing the route as presented here means the climbing is done earlier in the day and the descent is the reward.

From Termignon, follow the road out of the village towards the lower valley. After the sharp left bend just after the Doron bridge and the famous weeping lady war memorial, take the right-hand, rising track waymarked Red 5. Follow this gently uphill then down a breezy descent to arrive at **Sollières l'Endroit**. Turn right onto the road and begin to climb. The road climb lasts for around 800m before a track on the left signed Red 5 is spotted. This generally follows the road but is a far more pleasant option, with an occasional downhill section to break up the grind. The track then enters a pleasantly shaded forested section, which continues to climb.

After passing a road hairpin on the right the track splits and two options present themselves. Take the 'Aussois retour' option. This point will be returned to later in the day. The track gently undulates to a wonderful wooden bridge built for the winter cross-country skiing

Sublime single track on the climb to the monolith

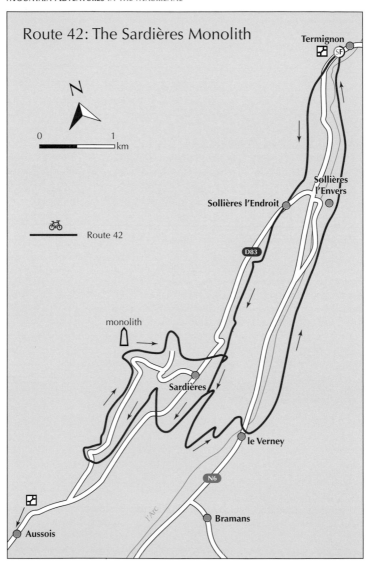

Route 42: The Sardières Monolith

0   1 km

Route 42

Termignon

Sollières l'Envers

Sollières l'Endroit

D83

monolith

Sardières

le Verney

N6

l'Arc

Bramans

Aussois

that is justifiably popular on this plateau. After crossing the bridge the route quickly turns to single track, which twists its way through some forest before joining forestry tracks again. The track joins a minor road leading to Plan de la Croix (not the D83 as marked on the VTT-FFC map). An option on meeting this minor road is to follow it into **Aussois** for lunch or a coffee.

Alternatively, turn right here and almost immediately turn left (Red 5) for some entertaining single track, interspersed with forestry tracks, which steadily climbs above the road. As the single track begins its descent, keep an eye to the right to view the **monolith** – a swinging turn joins the car park for it. The road would provide an easier option but would miss some wonderful but not too challenging single-track riding. Follow the road for a short distance before rejoining some wide dirt tracks with a few sharp turns; these trails are popular with walkers so care is needed. Before long the trail leads into the village of **Sardières**.

After turning left onto the road to Termignon (a speedy and simple option of 15mins or so) the trail (Red 5) takes off to the right and returns to the earlier junction. This time the 'other' option is taken and an exhilarating descent lies ahead. Long straight sections are interspersed with sharp turns, the surface is hard packed but stony so an element of care is needed. Eventually, the main valley road is reached at **le Verney**. Turn right then almost immediately left and left again onto Rue de Mont Froid. Red 5 signs seem to be missing here but it is the Chemin du Petit Bonheur. The trail is a mixture of wide tracks and occasional narrow sections, which passes the small airstrip (and offers a good vantage point for the climbing venue there) and undulates back to **Termignon** for a well earned post-ride beer!

The Sardières Monolith

ROUTE 43
Mont Cenis Circuit

Time	5hrs
Distance	40km
Ascent	1000+m
Map	3634OT Val Cenis
Start	Termignon village centre
Grade	Black

This is a long ride with significant climbs and is reasonably committing as there are few short-cut options. A very challenging descent will see all but the most technically capable rider walking for at least some of it, although the second part of the descent on rough tarmac roads is exhilarating and fast. A beautiful little church is worth a stop-off and a familiar finish along the Chemin du Petit Bonheur completes this epic ride.

Two options exist for the main climb of the day: one is through the forest on good forest trails; the other is to follow the road to gain the Col du Mont Cenis. This road is at a very steady gradient, being one of Napoleon's masterpieces to aid the easy movement of artillery into the Piedmont region of Italy.

The uniform gradient of the Napoleonic road over Col du Mont Cenis makes progress less difficult

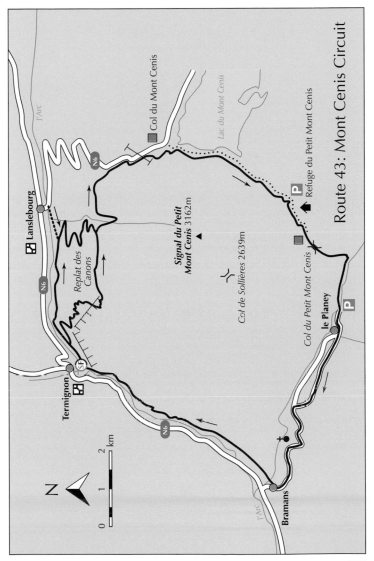

Route 43: Mont Cenis Circuit

Col du Mont Cenis

Lac du Mont Cenis

l'Arc

N6

Lanslebourg

Refuge du Petit Mont Cenis

P

Replat des Canons

Signal du Petit Mont Cenis 3162m

Col de Sollières 2639m

N6

Col du Petit Mont Cenis

le Planey

P

SF

Termignon

N6

Bramans

l'Arc

N

km

0   1   2

If a true off-road route appeals then there are two ways to gain the **Col du Mont Cenis**. Taking the Chemin du Petit Bonheur to the end of the metalled road in Termignon and then taking the right fork (Red 8) to the **Replat des Canons** will take around 1½hrs (unless it is a Tuesday and the ski lift is used). From here, Black 15 traverses the high mountainside, with some fabulous views and some sobering memorials of troops being killed in conflicts and avalanches. Alternatively, from **Lanslebourg** the Chemin du Petit Bonheur climbs westwards following Black 5 signage to climb to the same traversing track. This track gains the road by la Ramasse farm on the col road.

However the col is gained, a welcome descent follows for a short while. After passing the Buffa ski lift, take the rough road signed to **Refuge du Petit Mont Cenis**. This road descends steeply and then levels out for an undulating ride along the dead-end road, passing the refuge car park. Continue along the metalled road, passing a restaurant at the **Col du Petit Mont Cenis** and the very end of the road. From here the track becomes much more MTB friendly. The trail continues to be marked Black 5 and after a kilometre or so it begins to steepen its descent. A free-ride or all-mountain bike with longer travel and a rider with sufficient skills will certainly cope with the descent much better than an XC bike. The descent eventually eases off as **le Planey** is reached and riding becomes friendlier. The car park signals the start of the rough road and the end of the tracks. It is hard to imagine how Hannibal got elephants up the very path that formed this descent! The road crosses a bridge with a picnic site on the left.

As the road drops right after the bridge, the option of an older road offers an interesting and quieter alternative. This road (not the dirt track) runs parallel to the newer road but has some interesting landslip features along its length. The two roads merge after a couple of kilometres. This road continues to descend and it is easy to gather a lot of speed. The road can be busy at times and has some pretty serious drainage channels. The small **church** of

Notre Dame de Délivrance is enchanting and worthy of a short stop-off. More serious twisting and turning tarmac leads into **Bramans**. As the village is reached the route takes the first road on the right to pick up the Chemin du Petit Bonheur back to **Termignon**. A tough day out!

The beautiful Chapel of Notre Dame de Délivrance on the road back to Bramans

6 ROAD RIDES

The chief reason to cycle in the Maurienne valley is to become a real King of the Mountains. The passes here are world famous and will need no introduction to regular cyclists and Tour de France followers. Each climb has significant height gain, far more than anything in the UK.

Routes 44 to 48 are just four routes to consider; plenty more options present themselves to the intrepid and fit road cyclist. A very good little booklet, 'Guide Cyclotourisme', is available from tourist information offices, and gives a number of other routes to enjoy along the length of the valley. Most of these are in the lower valley but include the Col du Fer, Col de Madeleine and numerous loops of varying length and difficulty. Tours can be planned to cross various passes out of the valley and cross back into it lower down or higher to form epic loops. Many of these can be completed in a light touring style making use of the plentiful supply of hotels, gîtes d'étapes or youth hostels. Possible routes include riding up the valley to Bonneval-sur-Arc, crossing the Col de l'Iseran, descending past Val d'Isère and returning via Col de Madeleine having passed Bourg Saint Maurice and Moutiers. Another challenge could be crossing the Col du Galibier to Briançon before riding to Susa and making a crossing of the Col du Mont Cenis back into the valley. None of these are easy – crossing an Alpine giant never will be!

Sportif events are taken seriously in the valley and will see pro teams riding alongside visitors and locals

ROUTE 44
Col du Mont Cenis

Time	less than 1hr (ascent)
Distance	10km
Ascent	700m
Start	Lanslebourg

Thanks to Napoleon's engineers this climb is at a uniform gradient for almost all its entire length. It is a short introduction to Alpine cols and will take little more than an hour for an acclimatised cyclist. It enjoys ever-expanding views into the Maurienne, especially towards la Dent Parrachée. A café at the summit makes this a perfect easy morning route.

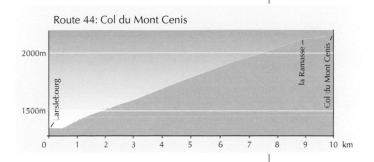

Route 44: Col du Mont Cenis

From Lanslebourg, the road is simply signposted 'Italy'. It crosses the Arc river and climbs out of the valley passing a road junction to Lanslevillard. The ascent continues in a number of very long zigzags, which mean the gradient is constant but the distance is increased to keep this easy gradient for horse drawn munitions wagons from the early 1800s. After snaking up the mountain the road breaks the treeline and a viewpoint with an orientation table are

159

passed on the right. From here the road gradient is less uniform and the farm and dairy at **la Ramasse** is reached.

The road continues for only 1–2km before reaching the restaurant at the top of the **Col du Mont Cenis**. A well-earned break here will restore energy levels before you decide whether to continue along the road to visit the Mont Cenis Pyramid with its small museum and further to the dam wall and views down into Italy. A rough road around the lake is a possibility for hybrid or mountain bikes but would be too much for a delicate road bike; punctures and a very uncomfortable ride are guaranteed. For the sadistic climber, a descent to Susa for lunch and the return climb are a significant challenge, as the pass from this direction is a climb of over 1500m, almost a vertical mile, twice that of the Lanslebourg side.

ROUTE 45

Aussois Loop

Time	2–2½hrs
Distance	36km
Ascent	450m
Start	Termignon

A circuit that can be completed in either direction and enjoys spectacular views throughout, this journey is a classic of the upper valley and makes a good training ride for those with greater ambitions. It passes the fort complex and visits a number of villages, allowing rest stops to suit. A short detour to the monoliths at Sardières is also worth adding into the itinerary.

Completing the circuit in a clockwise direction from Termignon means a long (16km) downhill stretch to start. This changes to a steady climb to the Monolith and then another long descent to finish. The anticlockwise alternative is a climb to begin the day, followed by a steeper descent to Modane before a 16km climb back to Termignon.

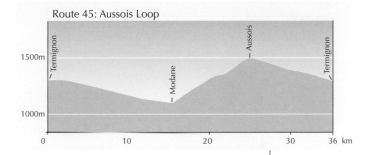

Route 45: Aussois Loop

From Termignon the N6 follows alongside the river, breezing through Bramans and sweeping past the fort complex as it approaches Modane. This is indeed an historic road, one of those commissioned and designed by Napoleon to aid his conquest of Italy. Some also believe it is the route followed by Hannibal's army on its approach to cross the high Alps. The Fell railway followed the Napoleonic road and the Tour de France regularly zooms along here on its way to either the Col de l'Iseran or Col du Galibier. The road drops from the forts to **Modane** and meets a small roundabout. Take the first exit (right), which passes under the railway and crosses the river. Once over the river, a right turn starts the long climb to **Aussois**. The view towards the high mountains is inspiring and will help to take your mind off the ascent. After 9km of ascent the village will be a welcome sight and the climb is complete, 450m higher than the bridge over the Arc.

After a refreshment stop in the village there are two options to consider. The first is the straightforward and swift descent to Termignon passing Sardières and Sollières l'Endroit before rejoining the N6 into Termignon. The second is to follow the road out of Aussois but at the 'gateway' sign at le Croix take the minor road towards the Monolith. This surfaced road contours the hillside to reach a car park and path to view the Monolith, an impressive 93m in height finger of rock reaching out of the forest. The road continues down to reach Sardières and on to the main road to Sollières and then Termignon. If the 450m climb wasn't enough it is possible to continue through Aussois to the barrages (dams) higher up the mountainside, this will double the climb to around 950m from the valley floor.

ROUTE 46
Col de l'Iseran

Time	1½–2hrs (ascent)
Distance	14km
Ascent	970m
Start	Bonneval-sur-Arc

The highest true road pass in Europe is a must for all roadies. At just under 1000m of ascent and a start point altitude of 1800m this means prior acclimatisation is a must if the climb is to be enjoyed. For cyclists keen to record a respectable time it is possible to have an officially recorded time on Fridays when a timing station is organised at Bonneval-sur-Arc and another at the col. Information and cards are available from the tourist information office.

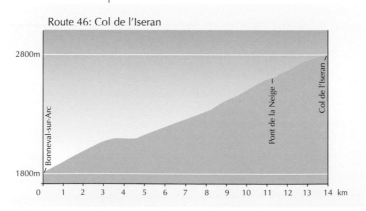

Route 46: Col de l'Iseran

From Bonneval the route is obvious; the road can be seen climbing from the village in an enormous zigzag. The road then bends to follow the stream and flattens off for a couple of kilometres, giving a welcome break for those finding it tough. For those wanting a good ascent time this section may be a challenge, as the temptation to spin the pedals easily is hard to resist. The road resumes its climb with more switchbacks and crosses a bridge before passing through a couple of small tunnels.

More fun on the way down but hard to keep your eyes on the road!

Pont de la Neige is crossed and the end starts to feel close. The road continues its relentless uphill battle, and at over 2500m the final climb and corners seem much harder than they ought to. The ground turns rockier as the col comes into sight and the top is finally reached. The coffee will never taste sweeter!

The return run will be thoroughly enjoyable and the views towards the Glaciers de Haute Maurienne will be a significant distraction. This could be the most challenging part of the day, keeping an eye on the road while taking in the scenery.

For the sadistic and ultrafit cyclist a 'double' could be contemplated. This would entail dropping down to Val d'Isère for lunch then turning around and climbing back to the col and descending to Bonneval. This would involve an extra 750m of climbing and is a committing decision as 'home' will then be over the pass.

ROUTE 47

Col du Galibier

Time	3½–5hrs
Distance	34km
Ascent	2100m
Start	Saint-Michel-de-Maurienne

Possibly the most famous of the Tour de France cols, this is a giant by any measure. Many UK sportives can claim similar height gains but never in such a short distance without any break. The upper reaches of the climb take you into a lunar landscape where the air is thin and the temperatures will be noticeably cooler. Be prepared, particularly if you plan to descend without meeting any support party at the top. A warm jacket will be very welcome.

The full climb begins in Saint-Michel-de-Maurienne and means crossing the Col du Télégraphe en route. A shorter version could be made by starting at Valloire to climb just the Galibier. This would then reduce the climb to 1250m and the distance to 19km.

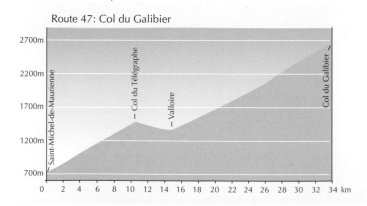

Route 47: Col du Galibier

From Saint-Michel-de-Maurienne the climb starts almost immediately after crossing the river, the route is well signposted, stating simply D902 'Col du Galibier' and 'Valloire'. The climb is a 13km ascent at around 7 per cent over the **Col du Télégraphe** before dropping for 5km to **Valloire**.

After a refuelling stop in this busy all-season mountain sports venue, the Galibier beckons. Owing to its fame and popularity this is unlikely to be a quiet day; other cyclists, motorcyclists and cars will be sharing the tarmac. Luckily, the French respect for cycling means you ought to be given room when being passed by vehicles and beeps will be in encouragement rather than anger! The road climbs relentlessly and passes through every geographical feature of a mountain landscape, from forest to bare rock, and snow patches can persist throughout the summer months.

The road passes the monument to **Henri Desgranges**, founder of the Tour de France, and struggles to the most stupendous of views from its summit. The Ecrins Massif ahead is dominated by the Meije's north face. From the summit of the pass it is worth the very short walk west to a tiny rocky summit and its view of the Aiguilles d'Arves.

And now for the descent! Care needs to be taken not to 'overcook' any corners, as a fall off the road onto the rocks is not to be contemplated. Neither is the prospect of cutting a corner short and meeting oncoming traffic head on. If you are being supported by a vehicle the option of a 38km descent to Briançon for a well-earned celebratory meal and a return over the pass in the car would be most welcome.

Beware the folk tale of meeting a '**white lady**' hitching a ride on the pass in poor weather; those who fail to offer her a lift are said to be unlucky on their descent, while those offering her a lift find she is no longer in the vehicle at the bottom of the pass.

7 WALKING TOURS

Following a route around a mountain over a week or two gives a real feel for an area; the Tour of Mont Blanc is probably the most famous such walk but is crowded in summer and refuges are often full, causing serious problems for any hikers without advanced bookings. The Vanoise is quieter (but still popular enough to provide a good number of refuges), with easy-to-follow paths and a much wilder experience. These routes vary from four days to a week and could form part of a two-week mixed activity visit to the area. As they use refuges each night, just a small rucksack and a loaded wallet can be carried, allowing you to enjoy the views without 15–20kg of paraphernalia nagging at your shoulders!

Kit list for a hut-to-hut walk
- Small rucksack – 30–35 litres; side pockets and a raincover are useful
- Waterproofs – Gore-Tex Paclite or similar
- Trekking boots – a Gore-Tex lined boot can be invaluable in the wet
- Two sets of socks – inner wicking, outer merino wool
- Underwear – two sets (wash them out in the evening, they'll be dry the next day!)
- T shirt – merino wool will last five days without washing
- Long-sleeved top – a warmer top
- Fleece or soft shell jacket – such as RAB Vapour Rise
- Zip-off legged trousers – these will double as shorts
- Trek towel – much lighter than a cotton one
- Tiny wash kit – share as much as possible
- Thin gloves
- Sun hat
- Warm hat (or Buff)
- Sunscreen/and lipsalve
- Sunglasses
- Trekking poles
- Lunch box and drink container
- Knife
- Camera
- Mobile phone – useful for ringing ahead to huts if not pre-booked, as well as for emergencies
- First aid kit
- Money – don't rely on huts taking credit cards
- Passports, EHIC, insurance details
- Maps, compass, guidebook, GPS
- Small headtorch

This ought to all fit into a 30–35 litre rucksack and also come in at under 8kg, making for light and comfortable walking each day.

The following route guides are outline plans only; they should be used to identify the correct paths, cols and refuges on a map but will

Crossing the permanent snowfield to the false col on the Tour of Méan Martin (Route 49). Ten years ago this was a glacier bowl

not explain every twist, turn, rise or fall. (All three routes are outlined on the overview map on pages 10–11.) A map, compass and experience are all essential trek companions.

All these routes celebrate the beauty of an unspoiled mountain region and there are many times were you can sit and wonder what century you are in – no ski lifts, no mountain bikes or paragliders, no other walkers for much of the day. Having such

a good network of refuges allows you to experience lightweight walking for days on end and enjoy good local cuisine in great company. Your only difficulty is in deciding which route to tackle!

If you fancy a longer walk then the 10–12 day route *Tour of the Vanoise* written by Kev Reynolds and published by Cicerone Press is recommended.

ROUTE 48

Tour of the Vanoise Glaciers

The glacial massif of the Vanoise is one of the largest in the western Alps; this extensive plateau is circumnavigated and reveals its size over the course of a week. Being at a lower altitude it is one of the most at risk from global warming, meaning denudation and glacial retreat are clearly visible. To spend a moment imagining the amount of ice that has melted is truly sobering. Old photographs in the huts show a much more glacial past and older maps will show the extent of the ice sheet which was present until comparatively recent times. The most recent maps clearly show the recent retreat zones: these are marked in yellow shading and the ground here tends to be unconsolidated glacial debris, loose scree or clean polished rock. Sometimes the glacier has been replaced by a permanent snow field.

This tour visits remote valleys and spends most of its time in the Vanoise National Park, and a range of native animals and birds are likely to be observed. A pair of binoculars will be well used. As its is a popular route, it is likely that you will meet a number of other participants following the same path, as well as people of various nationalities tackling the much longer GR5. Often these dedicated walkers are completing sections each year; the author met a Dutchman who was on his next-to-last year's stages having begun the route 12 years earlier!

There are a number of variants of this route. If pushed for time it can be reduced to six days or even five with judicious use of a car and driver, but this would detract from the feeling of success at completing a full loop.

The most commonly used start for this tour is Pralognan-la-Vanoise in the Tarentaise region, but given that it is a circular route access from the Maurienne is easily attained from either Aussois or Termignon. If the idea of leaving a car at the car park under the barrage at Plan d'Amont for seven days is unsettling (not a good security choice really) then accessing the route from

Termignon to the Refuge de l'Arpont is probably the favourite option. This is also a short day and will help if you recently arrived in the area and need some acclimatising. The significant climb means that although the route is short, it is not easy.

This variant doesn't stop in Pralognan-la-Vanoise but a diversion there to stock up on stores or washing is possible. Bear in mind that this route and others using the refuges are popular in the summer months, so booking ahead will be very important.

Goats being milked on the roadside near the Barrage d'Amont. This milk will be used for cheese production in the local dairy

STAGE 1
Termignon to Refuge de l'Arpont

Distance	7.5km
Ascent	1000m

Take the minor road past the campsite out of Termignon to the Pont du Châtelard and locate the footpath on the left. This path climbs very directly to join the GR5 long-distance footpath. Turn right and follow this to the refuge, about 2km.

Alternatively you could use the navette bus from Termignon to Refuge d'Entre Deux Eaux and then walk in along the GR5; this is an infrequent service so it is worth checking the timetable at the Maison de la Vanoise. This route is 10km in length with 350m ascent.

STAGE 2
Refuge de l'Arpont to Refuge de Plan Sec

Distance	14–16km
Ascent	505m

The destination is a group of refuges in the same couple of square kilometres: as well as the Refuge de Plan Sec there is Refuge de Montana, Refuge de la Dent Parrachée, Refuge de la Fournache and Refuge du Fond d'Aussois. They are all popular as they are on the GR5 and are also launch pads for some of the highest mountains in the area.

Retrace your steps from yesterday to follow the GR5 (if you took the footpath from Termignon). This path is a 'balcony path'; it follows contours to allow fabulous views down the valley and into the distance, without enormous ascents or descents. Some ups and downs are inevitable but nothing compared to yesterday's haul out of the valley. Most of the route is on the flanks of la Dent Parrachée and will reiterate the huge bulk of this mountain. The Ecrin National Park can be seen far away in the distance, along with views into the Maurienne and the mountains across the valley including Mont Froid. Around 6–7hrs will see you in the area of the refuges.

STAGE 3
Refuge de Plan Sec to Refuge de l'Orgère

There are two options for today's route, one gaining a high col with the option of an easy scramble to the summit of Râteau d'Aussois and its views to Mont Blanc, the other allowing much less ascent and a shorter day. An alternative to staying at the Refuge de l'Orgère, is the nearby Refuge de l'Aiguille Doran.

Via Col de la Masse (2930m)

Distance	10km
Ascent	725m
Note	After a period of poor weather snow may well be encountered on this route.

Follow the GR5 over the Pont de la Seteria and take the climbing path towards the col at the path junction. At the top of the Col de la Masse it is possible to follow cairns to the summit of Râteau d'Aussois (3130m), an extra 210m ascent and some simple scrambling reveals the summit and far-reaching views to Mont Blanc. From the col descend along the scree path which becomes increasingly solid and finally joins a grassy path and then the track leading south to the two refuges. A full day's walk at 7hrs.

Via Col du Barbier (2285m)

Distance	11km
Ascent	265m

Follow the GR5 over the Pont de la Seteria and keep on the GR5 overlooking the reservoirs to gain the Col du Barbier fairly effortlessly. The views are worth a break. Continue along the GR5 through Alpine pastures and old chalets, the roofs traditionally tiled in *lauzes* (thick stone tiles). The path descends through woodland and levels out close to the refuges. The route will take in the region of 5hrs so there is plenty of time to enjoy the views.

View across the Plan d'Amont reservoir to the Dent Parrachée range

STAGE 4
Refuge de l'Orgère to Refuge de Péclet-Polset

Distance	8km
Ascent	860m

The path, signed 'GR5 Variante', starts to the left of the Refuge de l'Orgère and climbs through the pine forest to join the GR55 at around 2500m. The Col de Chavière is in sight; early in the season some hard snow may linger here. Cross the col and enjoy the descent to the refuge. This is short day of only around 4hrs, which allows some relaxation/clothes washing at the refuge. It could also be possible to push on to Refuge du Roc de la Pêche at la Motte, which may be a sensible option if a visit to Pralognan-la-Vanoise is planned.

STAGE 5
Refuge de Péclet-Polset to Refuge de la Valette

Distance	12km
Ascent	875m

The path (GR55) descends northwards along the Doron de Valpremont to a junction at the hamlet of la Motte. Take either the path on the right which descends to cross the river and climbs to Montaimont, or the GR55 then a road which joins a path leading to the Chalet des Nants and climbs to the refuge. Either route will be round 5hrs in duration.

STAGE 6
Refuge de la Valette to Refuge du Col de la Vanoise

Distance	10km
Ascent	920m

Take the path north-eastwards from the refuge along the Cirque du Valette, passing to the left of Roc du Tambour. The path curves around le Petit Marchet and has a short length of cable to help on an exposed section. Now follow the path bearing right towards the col through the Cirque du Grand Marchet. ▶ Cairns help you keep sight of the path. At the path junction turn rightwards and climb to the refuge, a tough 6hrs in total.

The descent is steep and snow can lie late into the summer, so extra care may be required.

STAGE 7
Refuge du Col de la Vanoise to Termignon

Distance	Option 1: 7.5km; Option 2: 18km
Ascent	Option 1: minimal; Option 2: 250m
	(descent: 1450m)

A couple of options exist here. The first is to walk to Termignon via the Refuge de l'Arpont and complete the circle in its entirety. The second is to walk towards Bellecombe and take the navette (shuttle bus) back to the village. Which you choose will depend on how you feel about going down the long ascent you toiled up on the first day.

Follow the path to the two lakes, Lac Rond and Lac du Col de la Vanoise, taking time to enjoy the view down the Vallon de la Leisse. The path turns south and you meet a junction. Now is the time to choose: Option 1 will follow the path down and then right to reach the Refuge d'Entre Deux Eaux, then follow the improving road to hop onto the bus back to Termignon (check the times of services before starting your walk at the tourist information centre in Termignon as they are infrequent.)

If this feels like cheating then Option 2 is a complete circuit. At the path junction keep going straight ahead along a fairly level path. After about 1.5km the path joins the GR5 and continues to follow the contours to the Refuge de l'Arpont. Now the familiar path from a week ago is all that remains; retrace your steps to the path junction and then the descent of 1450m to the village and a well-earned drink.

If you have the luxury of being dropped off and collected by car then it is possible to start the walk from the barrage by Plan d'Amont and then be collected at the large car park at Bellecombe. This would shave two days from the walk if time is of an essence but does detract from the feeling of satisfaction of completing a circular walk in its entirety.

Another 'shortcut' that could be considered is from the group of refuges at the end of Stage 2, crossing over the Col d'Aussois and descending to Refuge de la Valette. This is a long day with significant climbs and so should only be undertaken if you are fit and blessed with good weather.

⛰ ROUTE 49

Tour of Méan Martin

A great walk with long valley views and (for a mountain walk) not too much ascent. Méan Martin is a large mountain block consisting of a number of summits and retreating glaciers. The French army can often be seen training on its high glaciers and on passes around the Col des Fours. Although beyond the remit of this guidebook, the summit of Méan Martin is a straightforward glacial walk and scramble from the Femma Refuge. Correct glacial travel equipment is needed, of course, and would add a significant weight penalty for the rest of the walk.

This tour is only four days long but will give a good flavour of these beautiful mountains and jump-start acclimatisation. High passes are gently gained and offer far-reaching views. An optional summit can be included and at over 3000m it is no molehill. Marmots and other fauna are almost certain to be spotted along the route and a range of flora will carpet the lower pastures. A short first stage to the Refuge de la Femma can make the most of an afternoon arrival in Bellecombe and shorten the

Plan du Lac and le Grande Casse

175

The Vallon de Rocheure near the Femma Refuge

following day's walk. Visiting one of the most picturesque ancient villages in France is an added highlight, and a night at the Vallonbrun Refuge will also be unforgettable. What this route lacks in distance it more than makes up for in visual appeal.

This route could also be started from Bonneval-sur-Arc; a night at Refuge du Plan du Lac would be necessary at the end of what would then be Stage 2.

STAGE 1
Bellecombe to Refuge du Fond des Fours

Distance	18km
Ascent	800m

An early start is recommended, particularly if you are not acclimatised. The route follows a well-marked path to the Refuge de la Femma (for description see Route 4) before your first real ascent begins with a climb to the Col de la Rocheure and its small lake. There are two options now. The more direct variation strikes off in an easterly direction on an indistinct and rougher path than previously encountered. The descent involves crossing numerous small streams and glacial debris. In poor weather, or for those with less confidence in their mountain navigation skills, take the path trending north-west, descending to a path junction where you veer right (north) and descend to a car park. From here the path climbs to the Refuge du Fond des Fours following the rough road which becomes a path. This is a longer route with greater ascent.

STAGE 2
Refuge du Fond des Fours to Bonneval-sur-Arc

Distance	11km
Ascent	450m

The path to Col des Fours is a consistent climb from the refuge (check the post box in the cairn to see if anyone has left a card or letter). From the col it is possible to take the ridge to the summit of Pointe des Fours (3072m), a scramble described in Route 13. This will add a couple of hours to the day. The path then descends to Pont de la Neige; older maps mark a glacier here but now only a small snowfield exists and is easily crossed in high summer. The GR5 'variante' link path is then followed down towards Bonneval-sur-Arc, where there are a number of accommodation options. Trekking poles will make the long descent less tiring.

STAGE 3
Bonneval-sur-Arc to Refuge de Vallonbrun

Distance	15km
Ascent	580m

A gentle start along the Chemin du Petit Bonheur takes you past ancient rock paintings at Rocher du Château on the way to Villaron. As you arrive at the old village of le Collet by the Col de la Madeleine the path starts an inevitable climb, passing the lovely slabs, Dalles du Mollard (Route 36). Zigzags keep you climbing out of the valley bottom to reach the beautifully secluded Refuge de Vallonbrun for a welcome drink and bunk for the night.

STAGE 4
Refuge de Vallonbrun to Bellecombe

Distance	17km
Ascent	660m

A fabulous balcony path above the treeline provides fantastic views down the Maurienne valley for much of the morning. As the path turn northwards on the shoulder of la Turra de Termignon a whole new vista of glaciers and peaks reveals itself. The GR5 continues almost to the parking at Bellecombe and the navette back. Ensure you have enough time to catch the last bus – times are displayed at the tourist information office in Termignon.

Another option is to descend from la Turra directly down to Termignon. Pick out the descending paths to Termignon from the farmstead. There are a number of options but beware that taking the straight down route along the ridge will involve a steep descent down a small cliff; there are cables protecting this but it feels out of keeping with a walk of this nature.

ROUTE 50
Tour of Pointe de l'Echelle

This five-day route crosses some fine cols, starting from the dams (*barrages*) above Aussois which form part of an extensive hydro-electric scheme that links with the Lac du Mont Cenis and the power stations lower down the valley. It encircles another giant of the area, the impressively pointed Pointe de l'Echelle. A taxi to the dams may be a good method of getting to the start point. Wild camping also seems to be tolerated here for a night but as the area is popular during the day it cannot be recommended as a long-term car park.

STAGE 1
Barrage, Plan d'Amont to Refuge du Roc de la Pêche

Distance	12km
Ascent	920m

Arriving at the dams in the afternoon will allow a pleasant 1½hrs walk to the Refuge du Fond d'Aussois and will break this stage into two smaller parts. A morning start will allow you to leapfrog the Refuge du Fond d'Aussois and cross the Col d'Aussois at the head of the valley. This path is well trodden, as the col serves as a high point for many day walkers. Continue over the pass and descend to Refuge du Roc de la Pêche, a long but rewarding day.

STAGE 2
Refuge du Roc de la Pêche to Gîte d'Etape du Saut

Distance	7km
Ascent	840m

A shorter day will be welcome after the previous day's long trek from the dams, although there is still a col to cross and so a significant amount of ascent to undertake. Retrace your steps up the valley on the GR55, then take the path up the right-hand (north west) mountainside towards the Col Rouge, descending along the streamside to the refuge.

STAGE 3
Gîte d'Etape du Saut to Refuge de Péclet-Polset

Distance	7km
Ascent	520m

Today the route encounters the Glacier de Gébroulaz at close enough quarters to shoot a roll of film (or memory card) or two. The path leaves the refuge and crosses the moraine to gain the right side of the glacier (note sides of glaciers are denoted left and right as per the flow of the ice). The temperature drop from the glacier will be noticeable and even refreshing as the climb continues. At the Col du Soufre the path descends to the refuge. Keep your eyes peeled for the bouquetin (ibex), throughout the day. Flora to note include the most famous Alpine flower, edelweiss, as today is a day of high mountain landscapes.

STAGE 4
Refuge de Péclet-Polset to Refuge de l'Orgère

Distance	8km
Ascent	360m

Much of today's walk is on the GR55, a derivative of the GR5. From the refuge climb steadily to the Col de Chavière – beware of long-lasting snow close to the summit as this is a north-facing slope. Descend to the path junction close to the Lac de la Partie where you take the left fork and eventually enter the woodland near to the Refuge de l'Orgère. As the refuge is at a road head and this is a short day, a descent to Modane on the GR5 would be possible, particularly for fit and acclimatised walkers, but would deprive you of a final day's walking. If poor weather is forecast or time is pressing this may be a more attractive plan. Nearby Refuge de l'Aiguille Doran offers an alternative to staying at the Refuge de l'Orgère.

STAGE 5
Refuge de l'Orgère to Barrage, Plan d'Amont

Today's walk, sadly the final one, gives two options, one the high route, the other the balcony route.

The High Route		The Balcony Route	
Distance	9km	**Distance**	8km
Ascent	1000m	**Ascent**	380m

The High Route
From Refuge de l'Orgère walk along the road towards the head of the valley until the road turns into a path leading to the Col de la Masse, which is crossed, and a zigzagging descent leads to the GR5 close to the upper end of the Plan d'Amont, follow the track right to return to the car park from which you set out four days ago. At the col there is the option of scrambling up the Râteau d'Aussois following cairns to gain a high point of 3131m and far-reaching views to Mont Blanc and a closer view of the Pointe de l'Echelle. This will add at least 1hr, more likely 1½hrs, to the day but an early start will facilitate this as a final highlight to the route and the views from the summit on a clear day will make it all worthwhile.

The Balcony Route
This follows the famous GR5 along the valley side, crossing the Col du Barbier before descending to the lower dam and a path around the reservoir followed by access roads climbing back to the road. It is also possible to continue on the GR5 to meet the descent path from Col de la Masse at the Plateau du Mauvais Berger. Care needs to be taken at the col to ensure the descending path is followed rather than the GR5, which is the more used route.

APPENDIX A
Route summary tables

DAY WALKS				
Route	**Distance**	**Ascent**	**Time**	**Difficulty**
1 Lac de l'Arcelle	9km	200m	3hrs	Easy
2 La Pierre aux Pieds	13km	1100m	6hrs	Strenuous
3 Lac Blanc and Plan des Eaux	6km	300m	2½–3½hrs	Easy
4 Vallon de la Rocheure	20km	200m	4–5hrs	Moderate
5 Pointe de Lanserlia	6–10km	600m	4–5hrs	Moderate
6 Hannibal's Crossing	15km	750m	5–6hrs	Moderate
7 Mont Froid	9–13km	750m	3–6½hrs	Moderate
8 Pointe de Bellecombe	9km	750m	4–4½hrs	Moderate
9 High Valley Walk	15km	800m	6–7hrs	Strenuous
10 Pointe de l'Observatoire	13km	1000m	7hrs	Strenuous

MOUNTAINEERING ROUTES				
Route	**Distance**	**Ascent**	**Time**	**Difficulty**
11 Pointe Droset	12km	800m	5–6hrs	-1
12 Crête de la Turra and Pointe du Grand Vallon	11km	1280m	6–7½hrs	1
13 Pointe des Fours	6km	550m	4–5hrs	1
14 3000ers Circuit	8km	800m	4–5hrs	2+
15 Lessières Traverse	8km	750m	5hrs	2 (PD)
16 Le Petit Vallon	13km	1100m	6–7hrs	-1
17 Roche d'Etache	7km	1135m	4–5hrs	1
18 Traverse of Pointe de Cugne	8km	910m	4–5hrs	1+
19 North Ridge of Cime du Laro	10km	800m	4–7hrs	1+
20 Signal du Petit Mont Cenis	17km	1300m	8–9hrs	2 (PD-)
21 Arête de Léché	11km	1350m	7–8hrs	2 (PD-)
22 La Dent Parrachée	12km	1650m	2 days	3 (PD)

VIA FERRATAS

Route	Time	Grade
23 Le Pichet, Lanslevillard	1–1½hrs	PD-
24 The Pinnacles, Aussois	40mins–1hr	AD
25 Guy Favre, Balme Noir	5hrs	D
26 Traversée des Anges	1–1½hrs	D
27 Montée au Ciel	1–1½hrs	D
28 Les Rois Mages	45mins–1hr	TD
29 Descente aux Enfers	40mins–1hr	D
30 Remontée au Purgatoire	1hr	D
31 Via Cordatta, Col de la Madeleine	2–2½hrs	III

ROCK CLIMBS

Route	Difficulty
32 Rocher des Amoureux	3c–5a
33 Sollières	4a–5c+
34 Rocher de Termignon	4b–5c
35 Blocs de la Madeleine	4b–6a
36 Dalles du Mollard	4b–6c
37 Drailles Blanches	4b–5b

MOUNTAIN BIKING

Route	Distance	Ascent	Time	Difficulty
38 Termignon and Sollières Circuit	7.5–18km	120 or 330m	1–2hrs	Green and Blue
39 La Girarde	8km	460m	2–2½hrs	Blue
40 Champions Loop	17km	660m	3hrs	Black
41 Chemin du Petit Bonheur	58km	800m	5–6hrs	Red
42 The Sardières Monolith	26km	580m	4–5hrs	Red
43 Mont Cenis Circuit	40km	1000m	5hrs	Black

ROAD RIDES				
Route	Distance	Ascent	Time	Difficulty
44 Col du Mont Cenis	10km	700m	1hr	Easy
45 Aussois Loop	36km	450m	2–2½hrs	Moderate
46 Col de l'Iseran	14km	970m	1½–2hrs	Hard
47 Col du Galibier	34km	2100m	3½–5hrs	Very hard

WALKING TOURS			
Tour	Days	Total distance	Total ascent
48 Tour of the Vanoise Glaciers	7	82.5km	5135m
49 Tour of Méan Martin	4	61km	2490m
50 Tour of Pointe de l'Echelle	5	43km	3640m

Pastou and his flock with Dent Parrachée in the background

APPENDIX B
Useful contacts

Mountain sport insurance
www.snowcard.co.uk – particularly good value for couples
www.thebmc.co.uk – for BMC members only
www.aacuk.org.uk – for Austrain Alpine Club (UK) members

Travel and accommodation
www.viamichelin.co.uk – travel planner with costings for tolls and speed camera sites included
www.hotelformule1.com – cheap accommodation near to motorways, bookable online and 24-hour access
www.sara-residences.com – link to apartments in Termignon
www.camping-termignon-lavanoise. com – Termignon campsite; includes online booking
www.vanoise.com/gb/fenetre_refuges/liste_refuges – list of the refuges and contact phone numbers to book direct

Mountain refuges
www.refuges-vanoise.com
CAF (Club Alpin Français, owners of many refuges): www.clubalpin.com

Refuge de l'Arpont   04 79 20 51 51
Refuge d'Ambin   04 79 20 35 00
Refuge du Col de la Vanoise
                     04 79 08 25 23
Refuge de la Dent Parrachée
                     04 79 20 32 87

To dial a French number from the UK, use the international dialling code **00 33** then the phone number, minus the first 0.

Refuge de la Femma   04 79 05 45 40
Refuge du Fond d'Aussois
                     04 79 20 39 83
Refuge du Fond des Fours
                     04 79 06 16 90
Refuge de la Fournache
                     06 09 38 72 38
Refuge de Péclet-Polset
                     04 79 08 72 13
Refuge du Petit Mont Cenis
                     04 79 05 88 67
Refuge du Plan du Lac
                     04 79 20 50 85
Refuge de Plan Sec   04 79 20 31 31
Gîte d'Etape du Saut
                     04 79 08 52 44
Refuge du Suffet   04 79 05 30 17
Refuge de la Vallette
                     04 79 22 96 38
Refuge de Vallonbrun
                     04 79 05 93 93

General information
www.hautemaurienne.com/en – English language website of the valley region. Lots of useful information and news of upcoming events
www.vanoise.com – the National Park website in French. Invaluable for

The ultramodern Refuge Fond d'Aussois with the old refuge visible lower in the valley

background information and links to many other useful sites in the area
www.valcenis.com/bienvenue-uk – great site for the upper valley, both summer and winter. Includes options to book accommodation online and weather information
www.guides-savoie.com/ – mountain guides office, Termignon
www.regis.burnel.free.fr/ – local mountain guide offering a host of summer and winter activities
www.guidesvalcenis.free.fr/ – the Bureau des Guides in Lanslebourg
www.meteo.fr – French weather forecasts online
www.via-alpina.org/en/page/1/the-via-alpina – a detailed site covering the various route options of the Via Alpina

Tourist Information Offices

Aussois	04 79 20 30 80
Bessans	04 79 05 96 52
Bonneval-sur-Arc	04 79 05 95 95
Bramans	04 79 05 03 45
Lanslebourg	04 79 05 23 66
Lanslevillard	04 79 05 99 10
Termignon	04 79 20 51 67

Equipment

www.aqua3.com – IGN map sales including a laminated version not available in France
www.optilabs.com – prescription sunglasses with a mountain/active sports design

APPENDIX C
Useful phrases

Pleasantries and manners

merci	thank you
s'il vous plait	please
bonjour	hello, good day
bonsoir	good evening. Goodnight
au revoir	goodbye
salut	less formal greeting 'hi'
à bientôt	less formal 'bye'

Navigation/route finding

à gauche	left
à droit	right
tout droit	ahead
la carte	map
la boussole	compass
le guide	guidebook
le parcours	route
nord	North
sud	South
est	East
ouest	West
une étape	stage/leg (in a walk)
le sentier	path (a footpath)
le chemin	track (similar to off road vehicle track)
la route	road
la crête	ridge
une arête	ridge (steeper than crête)
le col	col
le glacier	glacier
le sommet	summit
le lac	tarn, small lake
la jonction	junction
le cours d'eau	stream
le ruisseau	stream
la rivière	river
le bois	wood
le rocher	rock
le barrage	dam
le pont	bridge
la table d'orientation	viewpoint table (often on easy summits)

Accommodation

le refuge	mountain hut
le demi pension	half board
le dortoir	dormitory
SVP	common abbreviation on signs for *s'il vous plait* (please)
Je voudrais réserver ... lits pour cette nuit s'il vous plait.	I would like to reserve ... dormitory places tonight night, please.
Je voudrais réserver ... lits pour la nuit de demain s'il vous plait.	I would like to reserve ... dormitory places tomorrow night, please.
Je voudrais la demi-pension s'il vous plait.	I would like half board.
Je voudrais acheter ... pique-nique s'il vous plait.	I would like to buy ... packed lunches, please.
Nous arriverons à...	We will arrive ...
aujourd'hui	today
demain	tomorrow
hier	yesterday
lundi	Monday
mardi	Tuesday
mercredi	Wednesday
jeudi	Thursday
vendredi	Friday
samedi	Saturday
dimanche	Sunday

Weather

le météo	weather forecast
la neige	snow
le brouillard	fog
l'orage/orageux	storm (thundery)
la pluie	rain (in forecasts often *pluit*)
le vent	wind

ensoleillé	sunny
froid	cold
chaud	hot

Equipment

le sac à dos	rucksack
l'harnais	harness
le casque	helmet
le mousqueton	karabiner
la sangle	sling
le coeur	bolt
le relais	belay

Climbing/ via ferrata

Attention à la corde. Beware of the rope
*(used at climbing venues to indicate you are
about to pull a rope down or throw a rope
down).*

en tête	top roping
les crampons	crampons
la corde	rope
le piolet	ice axe
la broche à glace	ice screw
la glace	ice

Accidents and emergencies

J'ai eu un accident a …	I have had an accident at …
Ma position GPS est …	My GPS location is …

un	one	*six*	six
deux	two	*sept*	seven
trois	three	*huit*	eight
quatre	four	*neuf*	nine
cinq	five	*zéro*	zero

Nous avons … blessés	We have … casualties
Il/Elle a blessé …	He/she has injured his/her …
son dos	back
son bras	arm
sa jambe	leg
sa tête	head
sa poitrine	chest
Nous avons besoin d'un hélicoptère.	We need a helicopter.
Nous avons besoin d'une ambulance.	We need an ambulance.
Nous avons besoin d'aide.	We need help.

LISTING OF CICERONE GUIDES

For full information on all our guides, and to order books and eBooks, visit our website: **www.cicerone.co.uk**.

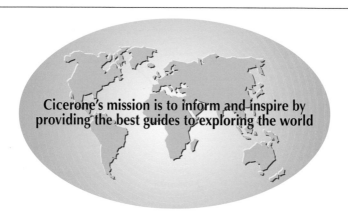

Cicerone's mission is to inform and inspire by providing the best guides to exploring the world

Since its foundation 40 years ago, Cicerone has specialised in publishing guidebooks and has built a reputation for quality and reliability. It now publishes nearly 300 guides to the major destinations for outdoor enthusiasts, including Europe, UK and the rest of the world.

Written by leading and committed specialists, Cicerone guides are recognised as the most authoritative. They are full of information, maps and illustrations so that the user can plan and complete a successful and safe trip or expedition – be it a long face climb, a walk over Lakeland fells, an Alpine cycling tour, a Himalayan trek or a ramble in the countryside.

With a thorough introduction to assist planning, clear diagrams, maps and colour photographs to illustrate the terrain and route, and accurate and detailed text, Cicerone guides are designed for ease of use and access to the information.

If the facts on the ground change, or there is any aspect of a guide that you think we can improve, we are always delighted to hear from you.

Cicerone Press
2 Police Square Milnthorpe Cumbria LA7 7PY
Tel: 015395 62069 Fax: 015395 63417
info@cicerone.co.uk www.cicerone.co.uk

CICERONE